Truths To Strengthen The Heart

Anthony Fusco

ISBN: 978-0615887012
ISBN-13: 978-0615887012

DEDICATION

This book is dedicated to my lovely wife who has filled my life with joy and happiness. She has patiently stood behind me and supported me as I have grown in the Lord and learned so much about his people and meeting their needs. Without her, my life would be empty and missing the greatest jewel that I have ever found.

CONTENTS

ACKNOWLEDGMENTS

Thoughts in this book are the result of insight from the Lord to meet the needs of people whom he brought into my life. Without their struggles and the opportunity of ministry that they presented to me, this book would never have been written. A special thanks to my wife and daughter who have encouraged me along the way. Thank you Anthony, for your support, love and continual prompting to put thoughts into print.

Practical Righteousness (Genesis 15:16)

One of my favorite portions of scripture is the account of Abraham receiving a promise from God and believing it. Many years ago when I struggled to settle the doctrinal issue of eternal security, this portion of scripture was key because when Abraham believed God, it was counted to him for righteousness (Genesis 15:6). What is important to see is that this took place hundreds of years before the law was given. Abraham's righteousness was positional. In other words, it represented how God saw him from the relationship perspective. Because of his belief, he was acceptable. As we know, there were future events that would take place when Abraham would not live according to God's will. The actions of taking Hagar for child bearing purposes, going into Egypt for refuge and lying about Sarah as his wife for self preservation were all sinful acts. These actions were unrighteous. Positionally, Abraham was acceptable to God and righteous, but practically, his actions were unrighteous.

Today, we believers in Christ are acceptable to God because we believe the work and promise of God's son. Because of this, we are in Christ. Daily we battle the world, the flesh and the devil and on more occasions than we desire or are likely to admit, fall to their temptations. We commit sinful acts and we too as Abraham become unrighteous at the practical level. We are still acceptable to God because we are his children, but our lifestyle at times is not pleasing to him.

As we go through trials, we must remember that before us is a great opportunity to demonstrate practical righteous living before God. It is quite simple and we fail to recognize it. Because we focus so much on the do's and don'ts of the Christian life, we fail to focus on our hearts.

To be counted with practical righteous in the mist of a trial, you must be like Abraham and believe God's promise and it will be counted to you as righteous living. You can do this. There are no lessons to learn, courses to study or prerequisites to attain. All you need to do today is live believing God will be God. He will work his will and he is closely attentive to your needs. His actions will be in love and will always be what is best for you. When you do, you will at the practical level demonstrate righteousness before God.

But let all those that put their trust in thee rejoice: let them ever shout for joy, because thou defendest them: let them also that love thy name be joyful in thee. For thou, Lord, wilt bless the righteous; with favour wilt thou compass him as with a shield. (Psalm 5:10-11)

An Upright Heart (Job 1:1)

Job is a name and person associated with trials and troubles. His success through great trial has been an inspiration to many. He was a man who was perfect and upright. Perfect in that he was complete and had all the qualities that God expected a man to have and upright in that his actions were the result of a righteous motivation that was within him.

Many think that Job's trial was his loss of family and possessions along with his loss of health, but that was the beginning. Job endured those trials along with the attack of his wife and friends. The latter trial was just as difficult as the former.

Remember that as Job lived an upright life, it convicted those around him in areas where their lives fell short. His honesty pricked the hearts of the dishonest, his patience convicted those without longsuffering and his love for God revealed the doubled mindedness of others. This was more than likely why his friends cast judgments so hard upon him. It was their payback time.

As we are in the midst of our trials, the enemy works on our hearts. What they do is press upon our hearts an emotion coupled along with a statement presenting itself as truth. An example could be a deep feeling of sorrow along with an accusation of "Why didn't God keep this from happening? At that point, our hearts could either embrace the deception and charge God foolishly or by our uprightness resist it and cling to the truth of God being faithful and good.

Through all of his trials, Job did not sin by charging God foolishly. Him being complete and upright even enabled him to pray for those who wronged him. It was at that point that The Lord turned him from being held captive by his circumstances. (Job 42:10)

Today, the Holy Spirit equips and completes us by his fruit, which enables us to respond properly to trials and overcome them. With the Holy Spirit's fruit and God's word to teach us in righteousness, we can experience victory as Job did.

Standing In The Trial (Job 4:12-21)

Trials are times of testing. They may test us physically, spiritually and emotionally. Trials are confusing in that the circumstances that they present seem to prove God and his promises to be untrue.

Although God allowed Job's trial to come, the author and instigator of the trial was the enemy. After taking away his family, possessions and health, he remained unsuccessful at causing Job to fail. Therefore, he continued to bear on Job's faith and righteousness by way of his accusers. In the same way that Satan, in Heaven, brought accusations against Job to God, he is now doing the same on Earth. In Job 4:12-21, we see that Eliphaz received a spiritual visitor who attacked Job's righteous living. Most likely this visitor was Satan himself. He lead Eliphaz in an attempt to destroy Job's hope (vs. 3-6) and to bear upon him with false accusations (vs. 17-21).

Since the Scriptures are for our guidance and admonition, we must recognize that the enemy will work in the same manner towards us as he did for Job. But how can we stand against such great accusations and overcome the hurt without caving in from weariness?

Anthony Fusco

While in a trial, you must stay in God's word. Truths that he shows you in devotion times will become the focus of your faith (Job 23:12). Without his word, you will not have what is needed to dispel the onslaught of lies from the enemy. Truth dispels lies in the same way as light dispels darkness. Without truth, you will become weary and eventually fall.

For victory, you must maintain your righteous living. Circumstances do not determine your measure of righteousness, but your faith does. Keep your heart clean and continue walking believing that you are right with God. If you fall, repent, confess and believe you are forgiven. Trials are not a punishment, but a manner to test or reveal the measure of faith and righteous living that you already have.

In the end, God will be glorified by your demonstration of faith and grace and your faith will be strengthen through and from the trial.

Sorrowful Meat (Job 6:7)

Before coming to Christ, I spent many holidays fellowshipping with family and friends while sitting around a card table playing poker. After the cards were dealt, I would glance at my hand and had to make a determination: should I keep the cards and play the hand or determine that nothing good could come from them and decide to fold or drop out of that round of play.

As we walk through life, unpleasant situations come our way. Situations in our lives may change drastically and to the point that we experience life in a way that we thought would be impossible and avoidable. Job stated this condition in terms of food when he said, "The things that my soul refused to touch are as my sorrowful meat." Because life is not a game like cards, we do not have the option of folding or tossing in our cards for a better hand. What we must do with this situation is make right decisions, live holy, trust God and move forward.

6

Some time ago, I knew a person who worked for a rather large ministry that had the financial bottom drop out. Because of that, there was no money coming in to meet his financial obligations. Instead of looking for blame or making hasty decisions, he decided to seek the Lord's face and allow him to lead. He remained faithful to The Lord, continued to serve him and moved forward. Through it all, The Lord provided a partial income through a second job and supplied the remainder of his budget through answered prayers. In the midst of the great trial, he experienced another set back with the starter in his car breaking down. The Lord blessed through the faithfulness of others the material needed and the labor for the car to be repaired. At first glance, the hand dealt to him looked pretty bad, but instead of throwing in the hand, he looked for God to get in and perform his might work.

For you, things may be looking pretty bleak, but it is not the end. The Lord wants to lead you, meet with you, strengthen you and provide all that you need through this time. Until then, pray for guidance to make right decisions, live a holy life by following the principles of the scriptures, trust God's faithfulness and take the next step.

Thy word is a lamp unto my feet, and a light unto my path. Psalm 119:105

I Want Out (Job 6:8-11)

As the dialog between Job and his friends goes on, what is in the heart of Job begins to manifest itself. As he sorts through the matter in his heart, Job comes to a conclusion for the answer. Job's solution is to cut himself off from the sorrow. He desires for God to bring his life to an end. It is then that he believes his soul will be able to leap for joy. He sees no hope in the matter or any expected end that should give him strength.

Because this event is recorded in the scriptures, we can see the end from the beginning. We can see that Job will be victorious over the trial. We can see that the trial may last for some time, but there will be an end.

We can also see the purpose for the trial and how his faithfulness in it will be a help and encouragement to untold millions. However, Job is blinded to these details. All he can do is trust the righteousness and goodness of God.

Our trials are similar to Job's. We are blinded to the purpose of our trials and the benefits that will come from them. God sees the beginning from the end and has allowed them to occur for his glory. He will be glorified by us as we see him lifted up in power. He will receive glory from others as we demonstrate his grace in action and our trials will be a part of the multitude of events for which we will give praise to God in eternity.

The answer for trials is not to seek an escape, but to seek for God. You can do this in a two fold manner: face the trial by accepting it as something God has ordained for your life, which he determines to be good (Romans 8:28; 12:1-2) and seek hope from the promises of God's word. Through these acts of faith, you will find God who by his Holy Spirit will bring comfort and power to you.

I Want Out (Job 6:8-11 Part 2)

While in the midst of his trial, Job requested that God would remove him from the burden and accomplish this by taking his life. As we know, The Lord did not answer his prayer and so is the case with us. The Lord does not solve problems our way, but instead follows his divine plan. However for some people when God does not respond as they request, they take matters into their own hands and attempt to remove themselves.

One manner of attempting to remove yourself from the trial is by taking action–regardless of how drastic–to resolve any issue causing the trial. People may utilize credit to remove themselves from a financial trial. If a trial involves work, they may resign or change jobs to get away from people or circumstance causing the trial. Others may remove themselves and escape the trial's pressure by altering their mood with drugs, alcohol, food or lust. What they fail to recognize is that The Lord has allowed the trial to fulfill his own purpose for their lives. He intends to use the trial to conform them into the image of his son and by removing themselves from the trial, they lose any progress that God has accomplished and will face a similar trial to begin the same work again. Sadly to say, others take their own lives. They hurt the people that they love, destroy their testimony for Christ and create trials for others. Their shameful epithet for life becomes "God is not enough".

How did Job respond? He petitioned God, but yielded to his sovereignty and divine will. For you, this is not an easy task and the journey may be long, but you will not be alone. His presence will be experienced in fellowship and he will carry you through when you feel you cannot go any farther.

Anguish of Spirit and Bitterness of Soul (Job 7:11)

As Job sat upon the ashes and scraped his sores, he continued to express how he believed his trial would end and comfort would await him upon the end of his short life. Until that time came, he expressed his heart and soul's anguish and bitterness. Many believe that spiritual people will never complain about the conditions in their lives, but that view is not accurate.

When we speak about our problems to people who do not have the power to bring about a resolution or enable us to bear the burden of it, then we are complaining. However, when we express our problems to those who can bring about change, we are problem solving. This is true for the home, work place, school and life in general.

There is nothing wrong with pouring out your heart and expressing to God the hurt and anguish that you are experiencing. Job expressed having anguish and bitterness. Because his spirit was crowded or held in a tight place, he began to experience bitterness in his soul. In most cases, bitterness is not a good thing, but for Job it was different. Usually when people face grave circumstances, they become bitter towards God and others. For Job, he was bitter or angry with the circumstances in his life

9

---

and not with God. Remember the scriptures say that in all this Job did not charge God foolishly. The Bible is filled with examples of people expressing themselves in this same manner to God: David (Psalm 55:2), Elijah (1Kings 19), the Widow of Zarephath (1 Kings 17/10-12), the children of Israel crying out in bondage (Exodus 6:5), Hannah (I Sam. 1:16), Asaph (Psalm 77:3) and the list can go one.

What we must remember is that when we pour out our hearts to God as we are in anguish of spirit and in bitterness towards the circumstances in our lives, we do not make accusations against The Lord or his people. Moses redirected his complaints away from God and instead attacked God's people (Numbers 20:10-11). Because of this, he experienced the loss of not leading God's people into the promises land. The children of Israel did the same by complaining about God and the circumstances into which he led them (Numbers 11) and their results were repeated acts of chastening.

Pour out your heart to God. Share the burden of your soul and continue to wait on him.

Psalm 62:8 Trust in him at all times; ye people, pour out your heart before him: God is a refuge for us. Selah.

God's Voice Amidst The Tempest (Job 9:16-17)

My father had been ill for some time. Heart disease had deteriorated him to a weakened state and he was slowly dying. It was only a matter of time. We waited. I was at a meeting representing a Bible college that I had worked for when I was notified that I had a phone call. When I answered, I heard my pastor's voice. After stuttering for a few seconds, he told me that my father had passed away. I thought I was ready, but the news still hit me like a ton of bricks.

When bad news comes, it hits us at the pillars of our strength. We are rocked at that foundation and the structures of our own making begin to crumble. Our works, knowledge, service and determination cannot help at that moment. The foundations are established in our hearts and as the

10

heart crumbles so do the foundations. However at the same time the Holy Spirit bears witness to our spirit of truth and our faith secures the truth structures that remain.

The testing time is when we believe in the goodness of God even though we cannot hear his voice. When we cry out to him, he answers or his eye is on us* just as it is on the sparrow. He may speak to us, but the devastation of the wounds in the trial make him seem to be silent. There will come a time when his voice will ring clearly, but until then, the still small voice is crowded by wounds from the tempest. The purpose for the trial is to remove our false securities and be strengthened in faith and fellowship with the Lord.

Until the trial ends or the voice of the Lord sounds clearly, bath yourself in the word of God. It is his written voice and can be heard at all times and under all circumstances. Pain cannot drown it out and it is the truth that the Holy Spirit will use to secure the truth foundations in your heart.

* the definition for answered contains the idea of God focusing his eye on something or paying attention to it.

Removing Pride (Job 14)

In anguish, Job describes the condition of his life. To paraphrase, he is saying, "My life of troubles is short and weak and I am nothing before God. Because I am a sinner, nothing good can come from within me. The boundaries of my life are set and as a slave I am bound to them." Job's solution for his life was death. In death, he would avoid all the hurt, pain and wrath of God until the appointed time that God calls him again. The Apostle Paul understood this quite well, but also recognized the importance and purpose for his life (Phil. 1:23-25).

This error of Job was caused by him being unable to see and understand the complete work and purpose of God for his life. The trials that Job was experiencing were revealing to him the nature of his life and this revealing was also breaking away any independence that Job may have placed in himself. Man's problem has always been that he thinks and acts like he is something and that he can live independent of God. Job's children lived that way and his wife as well. Because of Job's relationship with God, he continually submitted himself before him. Through these trials, God was removing him from any self reliance that he may have had.

In man, is a nature of rebellion and the cause of rebellion is pride. As all of the law hangs on two commandments of God: loving him with all your heart, soul, mind and strength and your neighbor as yourself, so pride is at the root of every sin. Trials are intended to break man of this prideful independence and to focus all praise and glory to God.

In the end, Job's testimony would bring glory to God and encouragement to countless believers. He resisted his pride and prayed for those that brought false accusations against him. This victory was eventually what brought about his deliverance from the trials.

As Job, we need to allow God's perfect work to take place on our lives. The trail may appear to be unjust, but we must remember that a righteous God always works righteousness. Until we understand exactly what he is doing, we cannot grasp the righteousness behind his works. For now, faith must carry us through.

Words and Prayers (Job 16:5, 21)

Many think that to be a Christian would mean a life of ease and that difficulties of life would be avoided. However as we know, that is not the case. Before being a Christian, we were enemies with God, but children of this world. We experienced difficulties alone and without God. After coming to Christ, we not only continued facing the natural trials of life caused by the results of the fall of man, but in addition, we became enemies with the god of this world and were no longer a part of this world's system. That standing brought oppression from this new enemy. Life for the Christian may have mountaintop experiences, but many more trials fill their lives. At any time, there are more believers experiencing heart breaking troubles than are not. With all of us hurting, what can we do to aid each other as we journey through the darkened times of trials.

The answer is found in Job's response to Eliphaz. But I would strengthen you with my mouth, and the moving of my lips should asswage your grief (Job 16:5). Job states that he would use his words to provide the strength needed by believers. He would seek to use his words to bring about a change in their soul to where their heart would experience courage, be established and with fortified strength prevail against the opposition in their lives. He would also use his words to either halt or hold back their grief.

In addition to encouraging others to strength with words, Job states that he would make intercession to God. O that one might plead for a man with God, as a man pleadeth for his neighbour! (Job 16:21). His prayer to God would be earnest as if to argue, convince or make a dispute. He would carry the burden of others in his heart and take it to God in their stead. This would be much more than adding them to a prayer list or mumbling a few words before God daily. He would pray for them as he prays for himself.

We too should do the same. As I look back over the decades that I have been saved, I am saddened by how little I have seen Christians in this manner help others, whether right or wrong, who were experiencing troubles in life.

Coming To The End Of Self (Job 17:11)

My days are past, my purposes are broken off, even the thoughts of my heart. Job 17:11

Once the trial had begun, Job's health deteriorated nearing the point of death. The enemy was not permitted to take Job's life, but he was able to smite his body and this writer believes he smote him until death was believed to be near.

Job's heart was still very much alive and continued to experience the devastation of the trial. As he neared the trial's end, he viewed his life as if his days were past or behind him. As he tried to look forward, he saw no plans: all that he had planned had been lost. Plans for his family dissolved before his eyes. All wealth to pursue other purposes had been stolen or killed. Nothing in the future waited for him. No longer were there even new dreams. The trial seemed to prove that everything in the past and future were lost. Job's only consolation was to get to the end and right quickly. No plans: just death. No hopes or dreams: just death.

However, he could not have been any more wrong in his views. Soon, there again would be laughter. Soon again there would be children born and wealth to finance plans and dreams for himself and the family. But until that time, Job needed to experience life when it appeared to be hopeless and in that state continue on in faith. By continuing on in faith, he was no longer living a life for his hopes and dreams, but instead living life for the sake of what faith wanted him to pursue. This is the outstanding Old Testament example of dying to self.

If your trial has crushed your hopes, plans and dreams. Remain faithful to him. With your own purposes dissolved, it is time to live for his plan. Bringing you to this point is one of the purposes for the trial. Without this decision, the trial and your efforts are in vain.

Have Pity (Job 19:21)

Have pity upon me, have pity upon me, O ye my friends; for the hand of God hath touched me.
Job 19:21

As people go through trials, we cannot see the extent of what they are experiencing nor do we understand the depths of their wounds and hurt. Job was stripped of his glory and crown. Friends, acquaintances, neighbors, children and his wife were all estranged from him. His loss was great and his pain even greater.

When trials come upon people, we are always so quick to believe that the cause must be some form of chastening or judgment. Why must we think so? Why can't we deal with them in love and pity as brothers in Christ? If their plight was caused by sin, should not our actions towards them still be the same? Are our hearts still so calloused by pride and legality that we cannot reach out in love? God forbid if we continue on in this way. Why is it our responsibility to point out another's sin? Are there today a group of people without sin who are able to cast the first stone of judgment? The answer is still, no. Then to reach out in love as Jesus did and restore people is the action that we should follow.

We are admonished to help the afflicted, pick up the fallen or cast down and in the spirit of meekness restore others. So if you see a brother suffering a trial for whatever reason, reach out in love. If he is being chastened for his wrong, God will perform his work. Our acts of love may be that which breaks the hardened heart to repentance. If he is suffering a trial for the development of his faith, your love will be an oasis in the desert of his trial. We would do best to allow God to perform his work and we to follow his command and example and perform our work.

Direction When There Is No Direction (Job 23:8-12)

It seems that the most difficult part of trials is that either for periods of time or for the entire duration, God cannot be found. He is sought diligently with the heart, but to no avail. His presence is not sensed and direction for steps is unavailable. His promises of being ever present and guiding our footsteps appear to be untrue. Those faltering in faith stumble, fall and choose to depart from him. Enduring without direction is painful, confusing and wearisome. What should be done?

At this time, faith heralds that God is in control. He does know the way that you take and a purpose greater than you can imagine or understand is being accomplished. Faith wants to direct you to the principles and statutes in his word. These are the lamp for your feet and the light that will shine upon your path. As Job did, take hold of your steps, keep his ways and decline not from following the principles of his word.

Decisions Without Leadership (Job 28:28)

Decision making is a difficult task in itself. Couple that with the confusion of trials and the level of difficulty escalates. In chapter 28, Job explains this by talking about all the hidden things of the earth and nature and how man has found them out, but wisdom is beyond him. It is hidden from all men and beast and all wealth cannot buy it. It belongs to God and God alone.

What do you do when you cannot find a principle in scripture to apply or implement in your life? Job explains it well, "Behold, the fear of the Lord, that is wisdom." You may not know what step to take, but the first thing you can do is step back, fear that you may go against the plan that God is working in your life, seek his face and proceed with caution. In Scripture, this is called the fear of The Lord. The second step you can implement is to depart from evil. Evil is responding to a situation in a manner contrary to God's word. Whatever actions you take that are not motivated by faith are sin. Romans 14:23 states, "For whatsoever is not of faith is sin." Our efforts to work out our plan or to deliver ourselves is always sin. This can be summed up simply with "If you don't know what to do, do nothing. Wait on God."

Walking Without Light (Job 29:2-3)

As a teen, my father and I went to the mountains of Pennsylvania for deer hunting season. Early in the morning of the first day, I made my way from the camp and through the dark woods to my post. It was an area some distance from camp. I previously had marked the trees on the way with a can of gold spray paint. In getting to that place, I experienced some difficulty walking though the cloak of darkness which wrapped around my small lighted area. Staggering and stumbling as I did, I made it safely. Many would equate this experience to the Christian life as we walk through trials. However, walking through darkness with the guiding of God's light is not a trial, but instead the experience of the redeemed man in fellowship with God. A trial is when you walk in the darkness without the light of God's presence.

While in your trial, there are two things that you must cling to. The first is to believe that The Lord will honor his word and one day, when his predetermined time arrives, will bring light into your darkness (Psalm 18:28). The second is to maintain righteous living. God promises that to the upright he will bring light to their darkness (Psalm 112:4). Therefore, dabbling with sin can hinder you from receiving this blessing.

Thanks be to God for the many blessings in his word. Not only are they a guide for times of trials, but also a strength to the weary and forlorn.

Desiring Vengeance (Job 31:29-30)

If I rejoiced at the destruction of him that hated me, or lifted up myself when evil found him:
Neither have I suffered my mouth to sin by wishing a curse to his soul.
Job 31:29-30

Some of the greatest trials that we experience are the results of other people's actions or sins. One of David's trials was the result of Saul's jealousy and pride. As the scriptures record, David continued to flee for his life from Saul and his armies. Another example was Elijah and King Ahab who was motivated by Jezebel. He also had to seek refuge as the king sought the whole land to find him and then after a great victory at Mount Carmel, had his life threatened by the queen. Both of these men endured the great trial of walking in fear and darkness caused by the sin of another.

Possibly your life may be the same. You may be sought after by those who want to destroy you because of the hate that is in their hearts. Others may have taken from you people that you hold dearly to heart. Others may be seeking revenge for righteous actions that you did which revealed their lack of performance in the work place and the list can go on.

What Job declared while in the midst of his struggle was that in all situations such as mentioned, he did not rejoice in the destruction of his enemies nor did he wish a curse to come upon them. If our hearts were to make such requests or to rejoice in such a manner, we would be just as guilty before God as them. God instructs us that in love we are to heap coals upon their heads and to allow God to be the avenger (Romans 12:19-20). That does not mean that he is our avenger or to avenge for us in our manner, but the one who avenges in his time and because of his righteousness. If we hold bitterness in our hearts towards those without, we will become consumed by sin. Allow God to perform his righteous acts. Until then guard your heart from evil.

Self Righteous Sin (Job 34:9)

In the midst of a discourse with his three friends, Job declares that a man profits nothing by delighting himself with God. This statement is so far from truth. His heart and ours also can be turned to believe it by looking at the lives of the wicked. Job stated how well off they were. Asaph, the Psalmist, also struggled with the same perspective until he went into the sanctuary and saw their end (Psalm 73:3-17). Circumstances may appear to show that there is no benefit, but there is.

For all ages, the Scriptures still declare that there is none righteous, no not one. Job may have viewed himself as being right in all that he mentioned concerning matters of business, caring for the poor, widow and fatherless and judgment, but he was a sinner and battled sin in his life. His position and testimony before God may have been that he eschewed evil, but he was still a sinner. For this reason, Elihu was angry. There is a benefit in living for God. However, the benefit may not be wealth, position or ease of living. The benefits in living for God are mercy, grace and peace. Our position as sinners warrants that we deserve the most miserable of lives upon the Earth and then to face death and the impending judgment of eternal punishment. Anything in life other than that should be considered a blessing.

As you face the trials that come in your life and begin to focus on what you do not have or fail to experience, make sure that you recognize all that you miss. You will never face death as the wicked, because the sting of death has been removed. You will not stand at the White Throne Judgment nor will you vehemently beg for mercy only to be denied and then cast into the Lake of Fire.

However, you have experienced his mercy in salvation. God's grace has worked in your life and you have grown and become strong because of it. How many times in the past has God spoken to you through his word and encouraged your heart? Each time that he did, you experienced his peace. Your trial may be tough and because it is a trial, it is not the result of your sin. However, your life is not righteous enough for you to say, "I don't deserve this." Praise The Lord! We don't get what we deserve.

Hope For The Oppressed (Job 36:15)

There are different types of oppression: physical and mental. Physical oppression is when a person uses physical force to manipulate individuals to do what they want or to cause physical duress so as to suppress people's actions. Mental oppression is when thoughts are communicated causing fear, anxiety, worry, depression or hopelessness. To some degree, each of us have experienced these types of oppression. An older sibling or playground bully could have physically oppressed or manipulated you when you were young or an angry parent could have done the same throughout your life. Sometime in your life and as a prisoner, you may have lived under the fear tactics of another: fear of failure because it was conveyed that you were stupid, fear of acceptance because you were told that you didn't measure up in looks or abilities, or fear of deserving love because you were treated as a useless sex object.

Even today, you may still find yourself living within the confines of the oppressive messages that were conveyed to you over the years. There are many who continue to experience this in their day to day lives and are longing to be free. The question is, how?

Elihu's discourse reveals part of the answer. In Job 36:15 he says, "He delivereth the poor in his affliction, and openeth their ears in oppression." Mentally oppressed people have received negative damaging messages from their oppressors. More than likely, these messages have been delivered over a long course of time. So long that now even without the oppressor present, their damaging message imprisons the heart and mind of the oppressed.

This passage tells us that The Lord opens the ears of the oppressed. It appears that in order for deliverance to come, the oppressed will need to hear and listen to another message other than that of the oppressor. The Lord will perform a work of grace and open the ears of the oppressed or enable them to hear another message. This message will be truth, which will destroy the lies of the oppressor. What is equally important as the message is the messenger. This truth message must come from God's word and be conveyed by God's people. Satan has been drowning out God's word to the oppressed for many years: even when they read the truth that they need, the oppressor couples it with lies and negates the truth's effects. However when the truth comes audibly by believers in Christ, it resounds like church bells announcing victory. The affect of truth will only last for a short time before the oppressive lies from their memory drown out the jubilant sounds. This process will need to continue and repeat many times before victory is won. It is called, discipleship. Sadly to say, this is where the church is failing terribly. Today, the church wants to quick fix everything. The method is give them a verse, get them active and clean up the outside of the cup. No wonder there are so many tragedies.

If you know somebody who lives under the dominance of oppression, be patient with them, go the extra miles with them, wait for them...love them.

I Abhor Myself (Job 42:6)

Wherefore I abhor myself, and repent in dust and ashes. Job 42:6

One day you will abhor or hate yourself. I am not saying that you will hate your life or the conditions of it, but that you will actually hate yourself. One day, when you stand in the presence of your great Creator, King, Lord and Savior, you, like Job, will see him with your eyes. It is then that you will completely understand all the workings of God and what he was trying to accomplish in and through you. You will see with great clarity the error of your thoughts, how your frustration and worry were unnecessary and how each time you either balked against God or tried to solve your own problems in life had thwarted his plan and set back what he was trying to gain with you. You will hate you. It all will happen when you see him.

Isaiah saw him high and lifted up and because of it, he was speechless and recognized how unclean he really was (Isaiah 6:1-5). In God's presence is glory and all that he is and is doing will be revealed. And you shall stand in awe and utterly hate the sinfulness of yourself.

However, we don't need to wait until death to gain this perspective of ourselves and God. If we fall down before him in submission and wholly seek his face, he will be found. We will not see him as we will in heaven, but he will manifest himself to us in a super natural way. When he does, you, like Job, will hate yourself or at least your wickedness. This was the turning point for Job. It was then that God brought the end to his trial, exalted him before his accusers, used him in intercessory work for others and then eventually blessed his life.

As much as we may think and greatly desire for our trial to come to an end, we more so need to have our spiritual eyes opened and see God. It is then that we will gain that for which we have been hungering and longing.

2 STRENGTH FROM THE PSALMISTS

<u>Psalm 1</u>

This first and very familiar psalm contrasts two types of people: the godly and the wicked. In the comparison, he shows how the one is blessed and the other will perish.

The word blessed is a word similar to the exclamation "O how happy!" Its source is different from that of the common word happiness. Happiness can have its motivation from two sources: internal happenings or external happenings. Happiness that comes from external sources is short lived, but that derived from the internal is long lasting.

Imagine the excitement of going to a large amusement park with food, games and rides. As you finally arrive and walk through the gate, your insides are tumbling with excitement. You spend the entire day taking in all that the park has to offer. You are happy! However, if you returned the next day and the next and continued to go to the park everyday, you will soon become sick of the park and the fun will be gone. You were happy, but the source was not sufficient to bring true long lasting happiness.

Now, imagine that you are with the Apostle Paul in prison. Food, hygiene and sanitation are drastically below health standards. It is in this setting that the Apostle writes the epistle to the Philippians, which most determine the theme of the book to be joy in Christ. How can Paul be so happy in a place like this? It is because the source for his happiness is from within. Inside of Paul dwells the Holy Spirit. He has a relationship with him, God the Father and the Son. Because his source for happiness is from within and not the world without, nothing can rob him of his joy. Try to remember how many times in reference to a party, get together or holiday, you have heard someone say, "Well that just ruins everything!" Their source for happiness was focused on the outside. During the Christmas season, does your happiness come from the glitter of the holiday or does it stem from your interaction with God as you praise him for loving you so much to come to the Earth and die for your sin. Does your happiness come from winning the church picnic softball game or that the Lord has been so good to you by leading you to a good church and providing you with close friends. These are a few of the many examples of how in every situation of life, we can look within or without for our source of happiness.

Many ask, "How can I have this joy?" It is simple and is stated in this first psalm. You must direct your focus away from the world, its philosophies and what it has to offer and look to the Word of God. As the Lord speaks to you and leads you to principles that apply to your life, you must meditate upon them: turn them over in your heart. It is by this manner that the Word of God becomes a part of your being. You will not only know the Bible, but you will understand it and it will become a part of what you are. Once you have this word deeply rooted within you, the many blessings concerning it will come.

However, if you neglect the Word of God, you too shall be tossed about as the wicked. Although you may have eternal life in Christ and will one day be with him, you can miss out on what the Lord has for you and instead experience life as the lost do.

The Lord Is My Shepherd (Psalm 23)

The happy life begins with believing that The Lord is a shepherd to us and by his sovereignty will provide what is need for our lives. To experience this, we must recognize him as shepherd and believe that whatever comes our way is part of his plan and is intended to meet our needs in a special and personal way.

When we live our lives away from his shepherd leading, we run to a fro in the Earth looking for peace, security and satisfaction. The places where we look will never contain essentials for our happiness. That is why The Lord leads us to a different place and causes us to lye down in it. This place where he leads is where we live without want.

As we follow his lead, he changes our emotional state. He restores our soul or brings it to a point of resting in him. The troubles of life crowd in the soul, agitate it and cause it to worry and fret, but as we lye down in his pasture, we experience security in him and the negative emotions dissipate.

In order for us to follow God's righteous leading, he must first lead our hearts. He leads us from the pasture experience with him to our life's plan designed by him. Because of the pasture experience, we are able to rest in the promise of his continued security. The security that we have does not promise the avoidance of troubles, but instead the promise of his presence in the midst of troubles. With him, we can fear no evil.

Whether we walk through valleys or experience abundance of blessings that the enemies are unable to thwart, it will be because of his leading and provision. This is the goodness and mercy of The Lord. We can rejoice in his promise, presence and provision in each trial of life, but we can only experience them in their fullness after we lye down in his pasture.

Prepared To Preserve (Psalm 61:7)

Psalm 61:7 He shall abide before God for ever: O prepare mercy and truth, which may preserve him.

God wants us to abide before him. When we do, we are settled in him. There is no moving or vacillating in our walk or hearts. Because God wants us abiding in him, he provides to us what is necessary for us to accomplish this by measuring out what is needed for our lives.

He grants us mercy for abiding. God does not position himself against us as we so much deserve because of our fallen condition, but instead reaches out to us in kindness and favor. As Esther approached the king and hoped for him to reach out his scepter in acceptance, we face the same situation. However the difference is that God has already placed his scepter of acceptance out to us and it always remains there. It is for this reason that he tells us to come boldly to the throne of grace. God also provides truth. Truth is something that brings stability to our lives and is worthy of our trust. All truth brings stability, but God intends to provide to us the exact truth needed to keep us stable for the storms in life that we will face today.

As you approach his word each day, believe that God is accepting you as you come to him and that he will provide something needed for today. You may not even recognize what it is, but what you need will be given.

Wait and Expect (Psalm 62:5-6)

My soul, wait thou only upon God; for my expectation is from him. Psalm 62:5

One of the most difficult aspects of a trial is to decide what actions should be taken. As you are pressed between a rock and a hard place, many thoughts and ideas run through your head: some are good while others are not. An internal battle rages and the confusion increases. During a time such as this, David admonished himself to wait upon God.

When you wait upon God, you cease activity. You no longer try to deliver yourself, work out a plan, figure out what to do or solicit aid from others. Man does not and never will have the ability to rule his life according to God's mandates. So to wait upon God would be waiting for power or instruction outside of ourselves. In other words, expectation would be waiting for God's tug on your heart.

Our hearts are tethered to him. This tethering or chord is the expectation of which David speaks. The Israelites pitched their tents around the tabernacle in the wilderness and remained there until the cloud moved. It was only at that time did the children of God pack up and move on. It is the same way today. We must remain where God places us. Remaining may refer to a location or the circumstances we are in. We move ourselves from his ordained place by trying to work out our own deliverance. What God requires is for us to wait or to stand dumbfounded and to be tied together with him. Being tied together with him is hope. It is the expectation that at any moment we will feel his tug of leadership bringing the trial to an end or showing us the next step to take.

Moses waited when he stood still. Peter waited in the prison until he was delivered by the angel. The three Hebrews, Daniel and the host of saints mentioned in Hebrews chapter 11 also waited. And you too will wait. You will do this because you see him as your rock, salvation and defense.

Wait on the Lord: be of good courage, and he shall strengthen thine heart:wait, I say, on the Lord. Psalm 27:14

Refuge (Psalm 62:5-8)

Some time ago, my wife and I were on a missions trip to the Dominican Republic. While there, we broke away from the rest of the group and ventured to see the island. At one point, we sat on the shore and looked across the Caribbean Sea. In the far off distance, we could see a storm approaching. Needless to say, the storm came upon the shore more quickly than anticipated. Suddenly my wife and I were scurrying along the streets near the shore looking for a place to take cover. As it began to down pour, we came upon a small cafe. We jumped inside and took our refuge from the storm. Although our hair and clothes were already somewhat wet, we were safe. It wasn't anywhere near as romantic as the movies convey, but it was memorable.

Trust is a word that is a pillar of the Christian life and is found countless times through scripture. The word trust carries the idea of taking refuge. We first trusted Christ when we took refuge in him and the work that he did for us on the cross of Calvary, but it doesn't stop there. God wants us to continually take refuge in him as storms of life smash against our hearts. It is in moments of refuge that we learn of his comfort, safety, strength and care. For David, he saw him as his rock, salvation, defense, glory and strength.

Taking refuge does not mean that we need to run to a church building or physically position ourselves at any specific location, but it means to place our heart or soul under his divine care. When we were trouble with our lost condition, we ran to him for refuge. Now he wants us to run to him for all troubles of life. We do this each time we pour out our hearts before him.

As you travel through your day and face the troubles that are certain to approach your heart, run to God and meet him in the refuge that he has prepared for you.

He Never Causes Us To Stumble (Psalm 66:9)

Psalm 66:9 Which holdeth our soul in life, and suffereth not our feet to be moved.

God, who keeps us alive, promised that he would not allow us to stumble or fall. Although trials do come, he will not allow them to over power us. This Old Testament passage is similar to Paul's writing in 1Cor. 10:13 where he states that our trials are not unusual to man, but that with them he will not allow them to be greater than we can bear. This promise has kept many from calling it quits.

What is so sad is that there are people in trials that have felt that they cannot go any further. They believe they have taken their last step and that the trial, which has no hope in sight, is more than they can bear. The truth is, they really are right. When you cannot see hope, every trial is more than you can bear. However, God is present with us in all our trials and is trying to bring us the hope that we desperately need.

The victory battle for trials is not won at the circumstance level. In other words, you do not win the battle of the trial when the circumstances change. You win the battle in your mind when you by hope can see beyond the circumstances. Trials may over flood your soul like deeps waters (Psalm 69:1), but hope is the rock that you can place your feet upon to lift your head above the tide.

Remember, God's plan is not for you to stumble. He is holding you steady and will guide your steps through the trial.

Rebellion (Psalm 68:6)

Psalm 68:6 but the rebellious dwell in a dry land.

There are only two ways to walk in the Christian life: either with God in his way or in our own way. Our own way may be the idea of another or we may make a choice for our way because of influences other than God, but it all comes down to one of two ways.

God's way is God's will and in God's will, we will find that which is good, acceptable and perfect (Romans12:1-2). However outside of God's will, we will find ourselves in a desert place: having dryness of soul, thirsting for joy, and longing for peace and contentment.

Be not quick to think that because you struggle with sin, you are out of God's will or rebellious. Rebellion occurs when we turn away, revolt or become stubborn before God. It is not an impulsive reaction to life by turning to sin. It is a stirring in the heart that decides no longer to follow God and to resist him from ruling, guiding or using us in his way for his purpose and subsequent glory.

King Saul was like that and his life demonstrated this truth. He fought God and became lean in his soul. Each step away from God led him into deeper depression, anger and greater rebellion.

Being stubborn is to resist that which we know is good for us and doing so only because of pride. Failing is not rebellion, but turning against God and determining not to fight is. No matter how difficult life may be, we will never be right to fight against God, who in love is leading us through the difficult passages of life so that we may know him, escape the pain of sin's circumstance and instead experience his joy and peace.

We must keep close to God so that seed thoughts from hurt, pain, fear and worry do not become a root of rebellion in our hearts.

God, Be What I Need (Psalm 68:5-6)

Psalm 68:5-6. A father of the fatherless, and a judge of the widows, is God in his holy habitation. God setteth the solitary in families: he bringeth out those which are bound with chains:

One of the things that I enjoyed as a father was to provide things for my kids that they needed or desired. It pleased me to see their faces light up as they opened presents or became excited about something that we were doing together. Some may think that God is the same way and that he wants to bless us with things that we need. However a biblical view of God presents him differently. God does not want to give you what you need. Instead, he wants to be what it is that meets your need.

He did not give the fatherless a father, but instead became a father to them. He didn't supply widows with a strong male defender, he became their judge and defender. God wants to do the same for you. If you are lonely, he wants to be your friend. If you face life in fear, he wants to be your security. As you face trials and wax lean in strength, he wants to be that strength. If you are confused, he wants to be knowledge and wisdom for you.

It is time to change from looking to God with your hand out and wanting him to fill it, to instead looking to him with your heart out so he can meet with you and be what it takes to meet your need.

Tender Mercy (Psalm 69:16)

Some time ago while working at a mental health facility for intellectually challenged children, a young boy posed a physical threat of harm to himself. After various attempts to de-escalate him, I needed to engage in a physical restraint. Between his youth and agility and my age and being slightly over weight, it was only a matter of minutes before I became exhausted from the confrontation. This best describes what takes place when I engage in spiritual conflicts.

Spiritual conflicts are beyond my strength. As stated by the psalmist, when conflicts come, my soul is overflowing and my feet are unable to stand (Psalm 69:1-3). What I need the most at these times is God's deliverance. Praise God that I can count on his help and aid to come. I am assured of this because it is based on his tender mercy. The word used for tender mercy was in other places translated as the word "womb". From this I can see that as a mother cares for the baby in her womb so in like manner God cares for me. As a mother's heart pangs or her bowls are stirred for her baby, so God is stirred for me. This emotional attachment is based on God and his attributes and not my performance. Therefore, I can be assured that he hears me when I pray and will deliver in his due time.

When facing trials, it is most important that you remember that the Christian life is not a matter of performance, but a relationship. The relationship is one of fellowshipping with God and should not be mistaken as a role of service. Serving God will be a quality of a Christian, but it is the result of a relationship and should never be the substitution for one.

When The Flesh and Heart Fail (Psalm 73:26)

My flesh and my heart faileth: but God is the strength of my heart, and my portion for ever.
Psalm 73:26

Life is more than we can handle and the troubles greater than we can bear. God promises to give strength for trials so that we may abound and triumph in victory. However there seems to be extended periods of time in the trial that believers seem to struggle without power. Why does this occur and how can power be obtained from God? Is there a prerequisite to meet?

God's measure for providing power is never based on merit or by measuring up to a standard. In fact, his method is the complete opposite.

As Paul stated in Romans 7, there is a battle that takes place inside of every believer. The battle is to cease from naturally doing wrong and fight to do what is right. During trials, we have that same battle. However the wrong that we do may not appear to be so evident. We usually look for the blatant "thou shalt nots" that are evident, but sins such as pride or self-reliance are just as wicked.

According to Psalm 73:26, the Psalmist recognizes God's strength when his flesh and heart or his physical strength and will fail him. What God expects from us during trials is to cease from evil. The evil that he wants us to cease from committing is being wise in our own eyes and trying to figure out our own way of deliverance.

Trust in the Lord with all thine heart; and lean not unto thine own understanding.
In all thy ways acknowledge him, and he shall direct thy paths.
Be not wise in thine own eyes: fear the Lord, and depart from evil.
(Proverbs 3:5-7)

When we cease trying to deliver ourselves, he gives us strength. This does not mean that the trial will come to an end, but that the strength we need will be present.

Peace (Psalm 76:2-3)

Psalm 76:2-3 In Salem also is his tabernacle, and his dwelling place in Zion. There brake he the arrows of the bow, the shield, and the sword, and the battle. Selah

Salem, a word that means peaceful is another name for Jerusalem. As described, this place is a place of peace and where God dwells. But how did it become a place of peace? God, who is omnipresent, dwells in all the Earth, but not all the Earth has peace.

In other passages of scripture, peace has the meaning of setting at one again. Much like when a person breaks their arm or leg and has the doctor reset it. Only after the resetting of the bone can proper healing take place. When trials come our way, our lives become in disarray or out of order. It is at these times that The Lord moves and his actions set our hearts at one again. Sometimes the resetting is done through promises from his word or his manifested presence as we seek him in prayer. There are also times when he finally moves and brakes the armaments of the enemy. Praise The Lord!

Salem was a place of peace because of what God did. You also can dwell in peace and experience it even before the actual deliverance comes. Continue to seek his face and he will set your heart at one again.

Wrath of Man Shall Praise Thee (Psalm 76:10)

Surely the wrath of man shall praise thee: the remainder of wrath shalt thou restrain. Psalm 76:10

At first glance, this appears to be a puzzling portion of scripture. How does man's wrath praise God? Is not the wrath of man his sinful way of acting out his will upon others? When reading this passage another portion of scripture comes to mind. James 1:20 says, "For the wrath of man worketh not the righteousness of God." It appears that when man is in his wrathful state, he is not working God's righteousness. Again, so how does the wrath of man praise God?

There is a difference between working righteousness and bringing praise. James instructed us that when we are in the flesh and responding to life's problems with wrath, we will never be acting as a part of God's righteous plan. However on the day of judgment, every knee will bow and confess that Jesus Christ is Lord. The lips of the wicked who are being judged will bring praises to him even though there is no righteousness within them.

Although there may be a prerequisite to work God's righteousness, the wrath of man can still bring praises to God. Throughout the ages, God has used both good and evil to bring glory to himself. Probably the best sample of this would be the life of Joseph. His brothers, who despised and attempted to kill him, found that although they meant it for evil, God meant it for good. Joseph was also wronged by others, but God in his sovereignty worked his divine plan and through it gained much glory.

The wicked of this Earth may treat you with wrath. Remember, God will use their wrath and the situations or opportunity that they create to fulfill his plan and bring him praise. He is not allowing man to just randomly and freely hurt you. We know this because he promises to restrain all wrath that has no purpose in his plan for you or his kingdom. (psalm 76:10)

Remember, God is in control. Nothing can happen to you without him allowing it and you must recognize that for everything that he allows, it is designed as part of his plan for us and to bring him glory.

Thy Way Is In The Sanctuary (Psalm 77:13)

The psalmist, in the midst of despair, looks to God for strength. He strengthens himself by looking back at what The Lord had already done in his life, but he is still confused and wonders if God has forgotten him. In the midst of the stirring of his soul, he makes the statement that the way of God is in the sanctuary. Some may think this to mean that if a person enters the sanctuary or a holy place, they will find God or discover what God is doing, but the view is incorrect.

The psalmist's small statement has some great implications. Whenever we meet with God, it will be where he is and the place where he is is holy. By meeting with God, we go to that holy place. A final truth is that when we meet with God, we discover him and the way in which he wants us to go. We still may not understand what he is doing or why he is allowing things or events to occur, but we will know what decisions we need to make, the things we need to do and how we must live and trust.

By meeting with God in the holy place, you place yourself in the position so that you may be in the way that he is going and enable him to lead you through the trial. However if you fail to meet with him, you will wander, struggle and be at the greatest risk of becoming a casualty.

Remember, meeting with God is not a duty, but a time of drawing close to him for strength, guidance and fellowship.

Hope For The Next Generation (Psalm 78:7)

Psalm 78:7 That they might set their hope in God, and not forget the works of God, but keep his commandments:

God wants his people to walk in hope. Living by hope is done when a person expects by faith that The Lord will perform a task, provide what is needed or manifest his presence in their life. It is not the "holding on by faith" or "hoping" God will do something. It is living in expectancy. Just like when you deposit coins into a soda machine and expect to get something out or flip the switch for a lamp and expect the room to be filled with light. So, when the believer expects God to do as he stated, he is living in hope. Depressed people do not live in hope. Anxious people failed to live in hope as well as the fearful, envious and frustrated. Living in hope is the spiritual condition that is the result of fellowshipping with the person who will be providing what is needed or desired. For the most part, all who are reading this lived in hope for much of their childhood. You lived expecting meals on the table, clothes that fit and for the electricity always to be on. You expected this without a thought. You expected your father to provide all of this simply because that is what fathers do. But had you known all of the financial circumstances that your parents endured, you would have lived in worry and fear, which are contrary to hope. We fail to experience spiritual hope because we live in the light of our circumstances. God desires for us to live with him as our father in the same manner as we did with our earthly father.

As parents, we have the responsibility to lead our children. One of the ways this is accomplished is by sharing the hope experiences from your life with your children. Many years ago, I worked for a ministry that experience financial peril. Christmas time was approaching, and I wasn't getting enough money to make budget let alone the added expenses for gift giving. I prayed believing and shared it with my children. As The Lord touched people's hearts, money began to flow to my family. With each envelope or card, I showed my children what God had done and was training them on how to live in hope. Another precursor to a life of hope is to keep out the destroyer of hope, which is sin. The fathers were instructed to teach their children the law so that they in turn may teach their children and not forget their God.

In order for the next generation to live in hope, you first must experience it.

A Heart Twisted By Imaginations (Psalm 81:11-12)

Have you ever known somebody who for years lived for The Lord and then came to a point of no longer following God? I have seen it countless times. How did he or she get to that point or what happened to bring about such a drastic change?

But my people would not hearken to my voice; and Israel would none of me. So I gave them up unto their own hearts' lust: (Psalm 81:11-12)

From this passage, it can be seen that what takes place when this occurs is that a person comes to a point in his life that he no longer hears The Lord with the intent of listening. He reads the scriptures and attends preaching services, but he is not hearing with the intent of listening for the Lord's voice or calling. A battle begins to take place in their heart and mind. Thoughts or imaginations of their heart begin to change the desires of the heart. After some time, the believer, who at one time panted after God as a deer pants after the water brook, now no longer rests content in The Lord. As the passage states, the Lord eventually lets them go to run after the twisted imaginations of their heart.

Such a sad state that can only be overcome by repentance, which will be essential for them to return. Since they have ceased listening to The Lord, they more than likely will only repent after The Lord brings some type of chastening into their lives and even at that point they can still resist.

If this is you, pray while you still can and ask The Lord to keep you from wandering any farther away from him. If this describes somebody you know, pray for them daily that God would have liberty in working on their heart and that God would grant them repentance.

In meekness instructing those that oppose themselves; if God peradventure will give them repentance to the acknowledging of the truth; (2 Timothy 2:25)

Parent – Child Relationship (Psalm 111:7)

Everyday, The Lord is working in your life. Regardless of whether you recognize it or not, he is. As your Heavenly Father, his works are governed by his attributes or in other words, his works are forced to stay within the boundaries set forth by his love, mercy, and holiness. Never are his works able to be unloving, cruel or sinful.

From this scripture, we can see that whatever he does will be in verity (trustworthiness), judgment (right) and sure (as a fostering parent). Stop and think, is not this how we strive to treat the children we love? Are not these qualities the same as when be grant or deny them permission, lead them in decision making, or correct wrong behavior? When they fail to understand and question your motives, how do you feel? What do you think? And what decisions are you forced to make because of it?

God, our Father, is placed in the same position when we question what he has brought or allowed to come into our lives. We question when sickness comes. We question when children fail to turn out as expected.

It seems that the greater the trial, the more our hearts lean towards questioning the Father's motives and love.

What we must recognize is that God, as a parent, is fostering or building us up. Yes, he wants to protect us and provide for all our needs, but sometimes the greater need is something more than tangible objects or a life of ease and pleasure. How he develops us to be thankful, to appreciate, to minister to grieving people, to be patient and to increase faith usually can only come through situations greater than our strength can bear, which we simply call trials. A life without trials would be a life that is not growing in the most needy areas of development.

So, as you think of the trial you are experiencing now or as you face new trials, will you respond to God in the same manner as your teenager responds to your decisions that they don't understand or will you, by faith, submit to his loving plan and allow him to do his perfect work in your life (James 1:4).

Light In Darkness (Psalm 112:4)

Who hasn't been through dark times of trials? Through the midst of circumstances that try our faith, we feel alone and cannot determine the direction we should go. I remember one such trial where I described myself as being in a boxing ring with the heavy weight champion. It seemed as if each phase of the trial was like being pounded with lefts and rights from the champ. As a boxer in trouble cannot determine up from down, left from right or even sometimes where he is, so my trial left me dazed and staggering.

Praise The Lord for his word and the wonderful promises that it contains. Psalm 112:4-5 says, Unto the upright there ariseth light in the darkness: he is gracious, and full of compassion, and righteous. God promises that for those, who are upright, he will provide light or direction for them in the midst of their trial. Most believers feel that they cannot have this or deserve it because they don't feel righteous. What we must remember is that righteousness is both positional and practical. Positional in that when God looks at you, he sees the righteousness of Christ. This happened on the day that you trusted Christ as Savior. Practical righteousness occurs as we confess sins committed and our relationship gets restored with The Lord. What I need in order to claim the promise of this Scripture is to have Christ as Savior and to scripturally deal with my sins as they occur.

If God's promises were to be based on our own righteousness or personal merit, nobody would ever measure up. That is why he says, he is gracious, full of compassion, and righteous. In the midst of the trial, God will deal with us by his grace. God's actions towards us will be motivated by his compassion and we can always count that he will deal with us in a righteous manner.

So while in the midst of the darkest of trials, remember your position, confess your sins and expect light or direction to shine forth.

There hath no temptation taken you but such as is common to man: but God is faithful, who will not suffer you to be tempted above that ye are able; but will with the temptation also make a way to escape, that ye may be able to bear it. (I Corinthians 10:13)

3 STRENGTH FROM PROVERBS AND PROPHETS

Trust In The Lord (Proverbs 3:5)

Proverbs 3:5 Trust in the LORD with all thine heart; and lean not unto thine own understanding.

I cannot tell you how many times I have quoted this verse to myself. I usually did it when I was at the crossroads of some major decision in my life.

As I look at the verse, I ponder what is meant by and why the Lord put the words "with all thine heart" in the passage. I had always thought that trusting God was a pass-fail matter. You either are trusting him or you are not. I thought, "If I am trusting, how can I trust him more?" It doesn't say, "Trust him with part of your heart" or even "most of your heart." As I read this passage, I paused and pondered for quite some time about "all thine heart". I came up empty and decided to continue with my devotions.

As I then read the remainder of the verse, I discovered what it meant. The key words are "Lean not unto thine own understanding". There are two ingredients that affect my faith: knowledge and understanding. Most people are willing to trust God based on their knowledge of the scriptures, their past experiences with God or based on others' testimonies or experiences, but this will only be with half of the heart. What we, as saved sinners, are good at doing is trusting the Lord to work out our trial and then we begin to ponder and plan how it can be done. We want to figure out a plan and then—because we have faith— believe that he will bless and deliver. Trusting with all your heart is believing that God can and then leaving it to him to resolve the problem.

The remaining responsibility that we have is to acknowledge him.

If he needs us to do anything, he will direct our paths. When we cease to look to him for direction and lean on our understanding, we do evil. Proverbs 6:7 states, "Be not wise in thine own eyes, fear the Lord and depart from evil." This is why the Lord tells us to wait on him. Psalm 27:14 says, "Wait on the LORD: be of good courage, and he shall strengthen thine heart: wait, I say, on the LORD." From this verse we see that waiting is a heart issue, because he needs to overcome a weak heart in order to do so. Those who do not wait on the Lord are not trusting with all of their heart. So, as you face the trials of your life, trust in him, acknowledge his lead and wait for his directive.

Happiness (Isaiah 55:1-2)

The things in life that satisfy come from the Lord and are free. In this day that we live in, it does not take much to realize that everybody is looking for something in their lives to make them happy. Many have sought happiness by purchasing new or additional homes, motor and recreational vehicles and have come up empty. Others have sought for happiness in an identity. Whether it be a sports star, gothic queen or body piercer, none find true happiness. Countless others have gone into debt in pursuit of finding something to satisfy, but happiness will never be able to be bought (vs. 2).

The source for your true happiness can only come from the Lord. He is not a depository of happiness that pours out happiness to those who ask for it, but he produces happiness in the heart of people who interact with him. Proverbs 16:20 tells us that the person who trusts the Lord will be happy. Psalm 1:1-2 states that our happiness will come by interacting with God through his word. As we interact with him, our souls will be satisfied with happiness just as our bodies are satisfied with food and drink.

Are you truly happy? Are you interacting with the Lord? The first step of interaction with God is by trusting his son, Jesus, as your savior. This means that you trust that Jesus lived a sinless life, but while on the cross, he took your sin and all of the world's upon himself and hung guilty before God. As a substitute, he took your place and all the punishment that it deserved and paid the debt that you owe God. If you trust him to be your savior, your sin debt will be erased and the Lord will come to live within you and begin to interact with you. This all begins when you call out to Jesus and ask him to save you from your sin.

If you already know Christ as savior, let me implore you again to set your affection on things above and not on the things on the earth (Col. 3:2). This redirecting of focus will again bring happiness to your heart.

O taste and see that the Lord is good...(Prov. 34:8). He wants to show you his goodness and the best news is that it is free to everyone.

Too Weak To Run (Jeremiah 12:5)

If thou hast run with the footmen, and they have wearied thee, then how canst thou contend with horses? ... Jeremiah 12:5

Most who read my writings live in America. Many in Russia, the Ukraine, and other not so free countries who read this may experience life differently than us. With the prosperity in America and the liberty that we enjoy, our lives as believers are not plagued with levels of persecution as our brothers and sisters in Christ experience in foreign lands. Most difficulties that we face are trials to test our faith. They may be financial in nature or be in the realm of health, child raising, marriage, abuse or pressures from work. I am not belittling these trials nor am I saying that these trials are not difficult to face, but most are not coupled with the threat of losing life, possessions or physical security. If we cannot endure the aforementioned trials, how do we expect to face the greater trials that await us?

Some may say that if life is going to get more difficult, why not quit now. Life will become more difficult with or without Christ. However those who are abiding with him will gain the strength, peace, comfort and consolation that come with him.

If you feel that you cannot endure, you must ask yourself why. Why don't you have strength? Why is not God leading you? Why are you not experiencing the joy that he has to share? The answer is that you are not abiding and resting in him. Your duty of Bible reading is good, but it is not abiding. Your scheduled prayer time may seem productive, but if it does not turn into a time of sweet fellowship with The Lord, but simply remains a time a reciting your needs and the needs of others, than it to is not abiding.

Strength for trials only comes by the hope we experience from spiritual interaction with Christ. Communion with him brings the peace for which our hearts long. Begin today to break out of the routine of Christianity and experience The Lord through prayer and his word. As you pray, pour out your heart. As you would share your fears, hopes, dreams and longings with a friend, do the same with God. He wants to hear your heart's desires. He wants to hear you talk of your fears, worries and struggles. He loves it because it is during those times that he has ordained that he would reveal himself to you. He chooses to move in a reciprocating manner. Remember that he said, draw nigh to me and I will draw nigh to you (James 4:8). This is his plan. We must approach him as Moses approached the burning bush. When we do, he manifests his presence to us and it is this interaction that brings hope and strength beyond reason.

Find a person who continues on in the face of the gravesite of circumstances and you will also find a person who has met with God in the private area of their heart. If they can, then you can as well.

4 STRENGTH FROM THE GOSPELS

Restoration (Matthew 20:13)

In Matthew 20:1-14, we read a parable about laborers in the vineyard. Towards the end of the discourse, Jesus reveals that some laborers were upset and murmuring about the master in regards to them receiving the same payment as others who began working late in the day. Because Jesus only responded to one whom he called friend, it can be seen that it is the bond that you have in relationships that will enable you the greatest degree of influence in restoration and not your position, knowledge or authority. When people are struggling spiritually, they will also be struggling emotionally. It is at that point in their lives that they look to others for the strength that they need to get through their issues. In order to gain their help and strength, they will allow that person to cross their personal security boundary. When this happens, they will share the private issues of their hearts and they will only do that with individuals that they trust. The question is, "Whom will they trust?" We can find the answer by asking ourselves, Who are the people we trust" and the answer is that we trust people with whom we have some type of a relationship.

Throughout my life, there were many people in whom I could trust, but there were very few that I allowed close enough. Those that I trusted had one thing in common, they demonstrated that they cared for me and had my best interest in mind. It wasn't their position, degree or knowledge about a particular matter that caused me to trust them: it was that we had a caring relationship.

Many years ago, my son made some terrible mistakes. On his own, he came to me for help. It wasn't because of my education, position or physical relationship with him that caused him to do this. It was because we had a close relationship. We didn't always have that type of a relationship. There were a few years that our relationship was strained, but because I recognized the mistakes that I made as his father and asked for his forgiveness, a relationship was redeveloped that later on would be the most important possession I could have.

Are you having trouble helping people or even getting close enough to begin helping? Forget the counseling books and instead begin focusing on your relationship with them. When the relationship is right, the ability and opportunity to help just falls into place.

Doubting Faith (Mark 4:36-41)

Those who make accusations against God for failing them have first failed in their faith. (Mark 4:38-40). The disciples were in the boat with Jesus and water began to come in to where they could not take on any more water without sinking. At that point, it would only be natural to be fearful. Fear is not wrong because fear is present when faith is exercised, but fear that accuses God is always wrong. Jesus asked the disciples, "Why are ye so fearful?". "So fearful" means they were fearful in this manner and that manner was that they were at the point of fear to where they accused God. The reason they were doubting God's veracity and accusing him of failing them was because they had already failed God in their faith. What I loved the most about this story is that The Lord did not hold it against them. Oh they received their much deserved rebuke, but he knew it would only be by him delivering them beyond their limits of faith that could make them be men of faith.

How convicting to think of how many times I have given up on people who have doubted me or even resisted my leadership. What I needed most then was compassion and understanding so that I could provided to those in doubt what they needed to become victorious. The second greatest commandment is to love neighbors as myself. When I practice the Lord's method of grace to doubters as he did, I am in such a great way fulfilling this commandment.

Testimony (Mark 5:19)

What you say and do in the midst of living your life reveals what The Lord is doing in your life. (Mark 5:19). After being miraculously healed by The Lord, the former maniac of Gadera requested to go and be with The Lord. Jesus responded to him with the words, "Go home to thy friends, and tell them how great things the Lord hath done for thee, and hath had compassion on thee." And that is exactly what he did. The results were that the people marveled. In short, what he shared with the people is what he had personally experienced with The Lord.

Today as you go through your day, your life will reveal what you have experienced with The Lord. If words come from your mouth that are not seasoned with grace (Col. 4:6), then you are revealing that not much has happened between you and The Lord. Griping, complaining, exploding, backbiting and gossiping all reveal that nothing is happening. You may have even had devotions that day, but the time spent was mere duty. That is why you must meet with The Lord, seek his presence in your life and expose yourself to his word so that he can reveal himself to you. When he does, your life will testify of it.

Remember, we cannot make ourselves spiritual any more than we are able to make our salvation. Both are dependent upon The Lord, his work of grace and our exposure to the Word of God. As we interact with God through his word, then his grace will accomplish in our lives what we will need to share with those around us and they too as those in Decapolis will marvel.

Be Not Afraid (Mark 5:36)

Most miracles resulted from devastating circumstances for people at the personal level such as the blind, crippled, those who lost a loved one, and others who had some form of disease. These individuals could have become extremely bitter about their circumstances, but instead of the circumstances driving them away from God, they drove them to him. Their great faith was not only measured by their belief and request for healing, but their ability to overcome the hurt from their circumstances and the accusations presented to them by the enemy.

Their success was accomplished the same way as Jairus accomplished his: he didn't fear but only believed. Fear has one enemy and when confronted by this enemy it has and always will lose. Fear's enemy is faith. Whenever you have exercised faith while in the midst of dire circumstance, you were also experiencing fear: fear that the finances would not come and loss would be experienced; fear that those opposing you would be victorious; fear that you would not be able to make it through tragic circumstances; or fear that your worst fears would come true. However, when faith was exercised, fear was replaced with God's peace.

The way from fear to God's peace is by faith. So the next time you are confronted with fearful circumstances, remember the words of Jesus, "Be not afraid, only believe."

It Is Not, But … (Mark 5:39)

God's work in our lives is based on what he knows about the end of a matter. All we see is the now and the circumstances that declare it. For Jairus, he had a choice in which of these two views he would place his faith: would he believe that his daughter who had been near death had finally succumbed or would he believe in the guidance of him who had done such great miracles.

If you were in Jairus' place, how would you respond? The question seems almost ludicrous because the majority of us would give our doctrinally default answer of follow The Lord. However when we are in the midst of the greatest battle of our lives, the answer is not always so simple. Questions of doubt and fear begin to enter the mind. Is God really good? Does he really care? Has he abandoned me? In the midst of that moment, faith must arise. Faith in God and his promises becomes hope or an expectation in that God will do as he promised. As Jairus arrived at the house with The Lord, he was expecting that his daughter would awake and not be dead. He was living his life from the same perspective as God was: in the realm of what he would do.

Living this life of faith is not something that just happens. It is the result of a life of fellowship. The farther away you are from The Lord in fellowship, the more difficult it will be to grasp life from his perspective. However if your fellowship is close and real, the task will be much easier.

What situation in your life is The Lord trying to tell you that it is not, but…?

They Were offended At Him (Mark 6:3)

Jesus' words, that a prophet is not without honor, but in his own country, and among his own kin, and in his own house, are ever so true. Regardless of his teaching authority and the ability to perform great miracles, the people could not get over true and accusative facts about Jesus. The people allowed the natural facts or supposed fact in the statement of Joseph being his father to keep them from receiving Christ. They allowed those details to offend or trip them up in their life of faith.

Today, we judge them for this and believe in our hearts that if we were there, we would not have reacted the same way. However, we do much the same. There are people that God has brought into our lives that we have a difficult time accepting their leadership because we too are tripped up by facts of their lives. Early in ministry, my pastor told that we should not allow people to see our feet of clay: in other words, don't allow them to see you sin. We don't have the liberty to have a bad day, lose our temper, shout at people, say unkind words or act in any sinful manner. The reason being is that people focus on following a man when they should really be focused on following God. When they see the natural man in their leaders, they get tripped up. They have difficulty following a position, but instead follow the man or in this case resist following the man. There is no such thing as a perfect pastor, perfect parent or even a perfect boss. What we must do is recognize the position that they hold and believe that God will lead you through those who hold that position regardless of their flaws.

Stop and think, God used Balaam who from the account of Scripture was lost. The high priest prophesied correctly about Jesus even though he was lost and the enemy of Christ. On a personal level, I remember clearly The Lord speaking to me about a major decision in my life. He clearly and without question provided the leadership that I needed. He did this through a visiting pastor, who at the time was living a lie, which shortly would be manifested. However, God knew what I needed and he used those in the office of his leadership to provide help to me. Later, he dealt with the man living a lie, but I learned something very important and that was to allow God to lead me through the authority figures in my life.

Parents don't have to be perfect in order to provide leadership. Pastors are God's spokesmen. He will speak through that office and if they become disqualified, he will remove them, but in the mean time, he will still provide leadership to his people through that office.

Ask yourself, have I resisted God's leadership because I have a personal problem with those in authority. If you have, you have fallen into the same trap as those in Jesus' day.

Follow the position and don't be offended or tripped up by the person.

How Much Do You Value Jesus (Mark 6:4)

God has chosen to work according to how valuable we perceive his son to be. When he was in his own country, the people struggled with accepting him as the Son of God. Their focus on wrong information about Jesus caused them to have little value for him. Because of that, he was unable to do many works.

Jesus marveled in that the people were in unbelief. Normally to marvel would be to stand in amazement about something, but in this case it is the opposite or to be amazed by the negative fact of something. It isn't natural to be in unbelief. Unbelief occurs because of the heart's condition, which hardens itself against truth. Stop and think: with all the great teaching and miracles that Jesus did up to that time, the people were still in unbelief and because of it, they did not honor him.

I have learned that the more I am in the world, the greater opportunity it has to affect my Christian view. If I become enamored with the world, it will affect my strength to believe, which will affect my heart and in turn cause me to value Jesus less. Isn't that what Demas did when he forsook the work of The Lord because he loved the present world (II Timothy 4:10). When I fail to honor The Lord or fail to see him as a great value to me, his work will be hindered in my life.

Did you value him yesterday? Did you guard your heart so that you would not lose his blessing or did you carelessly plug along through life acting and reacting in the works of your flesh? With Jesus, there is so much to gain and even more to lose. Guard your heart, thank the Lord for what you recognize that you have in him and then ask the Lord to help you see even more of your blessing in Christ Jesus.

And He Called (Mark 6:7-11)

There are two kinds of people: those who by faith have not accepted Jesus as the Son of God and those who have. The lost or those who have either not heard about Christ or have rejected him, wander through life incomplete and without a purpose. However those who by faith have received him have a purpose and calling upon their lives.

After being rejected by the people of his own country and kin, The Lord called disciples and with this calling came their purpose, ability, a focus for fellowship, and provision for their needs (vs. 11). Although this account records the calling of the 12 disciples, it is no different for you or me today.

God has a purpose for your life and with this purpose comes ability provided to you by his Holy Spirit. He wants to use you in the work of ministry. Years ago a pastor defined ministry as "God using man in his plan for the ages". That is exactly what he wants to do with you. He has a plan that has been in place before time began and this plan involves using you to accomplish things in the lives of others. God wants to fellowship with you in the work and have you become enthralled in the wonder of his person as you see him perform his work of grace in you and in the lives of others.

Many struggle with this because when they focus on themselves, they fail to see any strength, ability or worthiness for this calling. I'm glad to say that at no time has God's working in our lives ever been dependent on us or our ability: it has always been based on his grace and mercy.

However, if you don't recognize this or fail to yield yourself to him, then your life becomes more like those who don't know him or have rejected him in that you wander through your Christian life without his purpose and struggle to find purpose outside of God.

A Divided Heart and Mind (Mark 6:14-28)

Herod believed the accounts of history, Scripture and the power of how God worked through the prophets to the point that he believed John the Baptist was Elijah a fact that the Jews of the day did not recognize. He also believed in the resurrection of the dead. However because of his heart, the beliefs of his mind did not affect his actions. Herod is an excellent example of a double minded man: his mind was telling him to do one thing, but the longing of his heart would not allow it. He tried to straddle the fence and in the end, his heart won. In reality, the heart always wins.

Herod's heart longed for power, lust and wealth and because of that, his actions always worked to bring those things to him in an attempt to satisfy his heart. As I meditated on this, I asked myself, "Is my heart divided? Are my actions working to bring something to myself other than that which would bring glory to God?" If so, how can I change it or better yet, how can I keep it from happening?

The answer is simple, yet difficult. Simple in that the solution is a small act or condition, but difficult in that it is a battle to perform. The solution is to guard your heart. In John 14:15, Jesus said that we are to keep his commandments. Keep has the idea of "to watch" or "guard" and what God wants us to do is watch or guard our hearts from wandering away from him. If we are successful at this level, our actions will never be a problem.

When we struggle in our hearts because of a conflict between what we believe and what our hearts long for, repentance is the solution. When there is a struggle between belief and the heart's longing, the heart will win, but if we immediately respond to the work that God may do in our hearts, we have the power to repent. The scripture tell us that God gives us repentance (II Timothy 2:25). The reason that we have devotion time with God is so that he can give us what we need to keep or regain the victory. Devotions are a time of communion and not a task of duty.

So today, ask The Lord to reveal to you the condition of your heart and to give you what you need to be victorious. Prayers like that always get answered.

What You Do and Teach (Mark 6:30)

The disciples had been sent out by twos to preach repentance. After completing this task, the disciples shared with The Lord what they had done and taught. At this time in history there had been many who promised deliverance for Israel. The people could have followed any zealot or false prophet of the day. What made the disciples stand out from the rest was their performance of miracles: demons were cast out, the sick were healed and the blind received sight. After seeing these miracles, the hearts of the people were turned to receive the message of the gospel.

It is no different today. We may think that when we share the gospel with someone that their decision was based on our presentation, but I believe that to be wrong. Before the gospel was shared, there first was somebody's life who exemplified the gospel. It may have been a co-worker, friend, parent or family member. There was first somebody living the gospel and then somebody sharing the gospel.

While at work today, live the gospel! At home, live the gospel! To your neighbors, live the gospel! You may later have the opportunity to share the gospel or it may be accomplished by somebody else, but for the sake of Christ and his work of grace, live it.

Stop and think, who lived the gospel for you to see before you came to Christ?

Dear Lord, thank you for giving me the strength and opportunity to live the message of the gospel. Please help me today to recognize the opportunities that you have placed before me and to share the wonder that you are doing in my life.

For Their Heart Was Hardened (Mark 6:50-52)

Have you ever had a problem that whenever you thought of it, your heart just quivered inside? You may have tried to push the thought of it away, but in no time you were thinking about it again and again your heart trembled. The disciples experienced that same type of fear in their hearts as they saw The Lord walking on the sea. The scriptures describe their hearts' condition as if it were boiling water. From that definition, we can see that trembling fear over took them.

When The Lord said, "Be of good cheer: it is I; be not afraid" and then entered the ship, the disciples were dumbfounded. The Bible says that the reason for this was because their hearts were hardened. When did they become hard and how did it happen with just a short time earlier they saw the great miracle of the feeding of the five thousand? Their hearts must have become hard while in the midst of being alone on the sea and battling the storm. As the battle raged and fearful thoughts entered their minds, their hearts became hardened: maybe to the point of faulting or accusing God.

Have you ever been there? Whether you accused God or not, we all have experienced situations that have gripped our hearts with fear. The way to keep from failing God by developing a hard heart is to remember the miracles that he has already done in your life. The disciples' hearts were hard because they considered not the miracle of the loaves or they did not put together (consider) the past miracle with the current trial.

When trouble comes, look back at what God has done in your life. Remember the answered prayers. Remember the sweet times of fellowship that you have had. Remember the strength that he has provided to you as you walked through troubled valleys. If you don't, you will forget his goodness, you will focus on the trial and your heart will become hard and with each time that the fear returns, your heart will become even more hard.

Father, my heart is afraid. These circumstances are greater than me and I need your help. I know that you are good and that as part of your plan to strengthen me and to enable me to see your greatness, you have allowed this trial to occur. Thank you for being good to me. I remember the times that you have helped me in the past and I am always amazed by your deliverance. Thank you, God, for loving and caring for me.

The Effects Of Your Testimony (Mark 6:56)

Jesus' fame was growing. As he exited the ship, the people of the region recognized who he was and began to gather from all parts of the city those who are sick. They placed them along the streets in hopes that he would heal them. The Scriptures also record that people were seeking him so that they may touch but the hem of his garment and that all who touched it were healed.

What an amazing testimony. Where did the people get the idea that Jesus did not need to perform some healing action, but that by touching his garment they could be healed? It came from a sickly woman's testimony in that after spending all her wealth on doctors for healing and yet remained sick, she secretly approached Jesus believing that if she but touched his garment, she would be healed (Mark 5:27-29). Because of her faith, many others were exercising the same faith.

This is the demonstration of what a testimony can do. All of us have one. Some people's testimonies are good and others have poor testimonies. Some have testimonies where their faith enabled them to accomplish great things or overcome huge obstacles. While others seemed only the need to exercise faith in less critical situations. But in all truth, each time a person exercises faith, they are accomplishing something great.

The marvelous part of the story is how effectual the testimony was of the woman who touched the garment of Jesus. Her testimony far out reached the expectations of her decision that day. She did not act in hopes of influencing others, but her life did.

Ask yourself, what kind of a testimony do I have? How far is my testimony reaching? What does The Lord think of my testimony? What testimony am I developing as I go through my current trials? Who is watching my testimony and who will be successful through their trails after seeing my testimony? After answering these questions, I hope you recognize that your testimony has a greater influence for Christ than you think.

Lips Versus The Heart (Mark 7:6)

The measure of how much you honor God is not determined by the out pouring of your lips, but by the fruit of your the heart. I heard somebody say that the tongue is the dip stick of the heart. What they meant was that as you can check the internal fluids of an engine and determine its level of care by checking the oil dip stick, you could do the same by checking the heart of man by what he says. The phrase may seem good, but it is an inaccurate statement.

According to God, you should not go by what a persons says to determine the condition of the heart. Words are easy to say and religious works of the flesh are not battled by the flesh or the enemy, but godly fruit always faces opposition. If you want to check on your spiritual condition, measure how often you get angry, or what response you have in your heart when you hear the name of a person who wronged you. Count the times you said words that should have been halted, thought lewd thoughts that should have been shunned, envied a peer or looked down on someone.

How far away is your heart from God? The true way of measuring is to take inventory of whether the fruit of the Spirit is in your life. Love, joy, peace, long suffering, gentleness, goodness, faith, meekness and temperance are all manifestations of the Holy Spirit. Your measure of spirituality is determined by how much these fruit are manifested in your life and not the words that you say.

Humility Diverts Blessings To You (Mark 7:26-29)

A Greek woman from Syria came to Jesus because her daughter was demon possessed. Because she was Greek, she was not a part of Israel. During Christ's ministry, the ministry focus was for the lost house of Israel and her being a gentile placed her in the lowest of categories in the social system: low because the Gentiles did not know God and their lifestyle was idolatrous and a sinful abomination to God. With all that said, here she was seeking help from God himself.

With her being on the out with God, how did she get him to grant the request that she made by faith? She accomplished it because she was humble. The Lord pointed out her gentile condition and that it would be wrong to cast the Jew's bread to dogs or to her and her people. Her reply was not defensive, but instead in agreement with what he said and that her only possible right would be in the carelessness of the Jews with receiving the blessing of the Gospel of Christ. Her humble answer brought her the blessing she desired.

How often have you thought that you didn't deserve the type of treatment you were getting from God or that you deserve better than what life had brought your way? How often have you thought you were more in line to receive blessings because of your laundry list of do's and don'ts that you keep. If I learned anything in my life, I have learned that as I grow in Christ, I see myself as more sinful instead of less. On anybody's best day, they will never measure up to a position of deserving blessings from God. However two things are essential for blessings to be obtained: believing faith that God can and wants to bless you and humility in your heart as evidenced by you seeing yourself more as how God sees you.

The gentile woman had both ingredients: she went to Christ and petitioned him to cast out the demon and she humbly accepted statements about her from The Lord as being true.

Are you humble?

If You Want It, You Must Tarry (Mark 8:1-3)

The crowd was large. Jesus had been healing and teaching for days. What supplies had been brought were gone, but the people stayed. Why? Was it because they believed he would provide food with a miracle? That was not very likely the reason, because the disciples, who were closest to Jesus, were still struggling in that area. So, why did they stay?

It appears that on the occasions when crowds gathered to Jesus, it was because they were in need of miracles. Whether they lined the streets with the sick or people for themselves journeyed to where Jesus was, the purpose was for miraculous healing. As they crowded to Jesus, some were still waiting for their chance to be healed. This lingering lasted into the third day. As time passed and supplies ran out, they had a choice to make: leave for food and miss the healing or endure without. For them, the greater need was the miraculous. They planned on enduring without food for the opportunity to have their greater need met.

As a child of God, you face the same situation today. You are not necessarily away in a desert place with Jesus far away from food, but in the midst of life's trials, you are like in a desert place without power and definitely without provision. As time lingers on, what will you do? Will your emotional needs or desires blinded you from the hope of the miraculous. If so, you will remove yourself from sitting at the feet of Jesus and attempt to deliver yourself or you will give up in despair. But if you choose to remain, his power will be displayed. You will see the miracle that you need. It may not be the miracle that you want, but it will be what you need. All you need to do, is tarry. Tarry a little longer. Tarry with the hope of his presence and tarry with the promise of his comfort.

Psalm 46:5 God is in the midst of her; she shall not be moved: God shall help her, and that right early.

Direction Versus a Sign (Mark 8:11-12)

Seeking direction from God is not requiring from him a sign. Those who are seeking guidance have faith that needs direction and the sign seekers, like the Pharisees, have a hardened, adulterous heart that needs repentance. Matthew 12:38-39

When you need a sign to create or strengthen faith, it is a sin because you are testing God. In reality, you are testing to see if he is listening and still present as he said he would be. On the other hand, if you need a sign to provide direction or to confirm what you by faith believe to be God's will, it is not sin, but a manner of seeking his face.

Many years ago, I was in the midst of a trial that had lasted for a few years. My strength was waxing week and I was becoming discouraged. After praying for some period of time and also weeping, I asked The Lord for a sign to let me know how much further I would need to go. At that point, I really thought myself to be spiritual. I then picked up my bible and with my thumb flipped open to a random spot. I looked down and read, "But he answered and said unto them, An evil and adulterous generation seeketh after a sign." I closed the bible and in tears cried out to God and asked for forgiveness. What had I done wrong? I was testing God in order to get something to convince me to have faith. Had he done something, my faith would have been in the event and not directly dependent upon him.

It isn't wrong to seek guidance from God. By seeking guidance, we are really seeking his wisdom. The scriptures tell us to ask for wisdom and for those who seek it, he will not upbraid or rail against them for it (James 1:5).

Taking Up Your Cross (Mark 8:34-38)

Over the many years of being a Christian, I have heard messages preached on this topic. Many with the greatest of intentions have tried to identify the meaning of this passage. They have focused on the cross and its meaning and with that understood, they try to parallel the meaning of the cross to the life of a Christian. They held that the cross represented a burden carried for the good of others. Some saw it as a representative of death and that bearing the cross would be accomplished by living a life dead to self. Each of these ideas for application are important aspects of the Christian life, but are not a true representative of this passage's meaning.

The events in this passage contain a conversation with the disciples about whom the people and the disciples believed Jesus to be. While speaking, he admonished them about following or associating themselves with him and not trying to save or protect their own lives and then he makes this statement, "Whosoever therefore shall be ashamed of me and of my words in this adulterous and sinful generation; of him also shall the Son of man be ashamed, when he cometh in the glory of his Father with the holy angels." From this passage, it appears to be that taking up your cross is to identify yourself with Jesus (following Jesus) and not to be ashamed of Him.

What would make a person be ashamed of being identified with Jesus? People become ashamed of Jesus when they become concerned about what others think of them. That is what causes them to cave in to pressures among peers or at work. They are afraid to resist gossip, dirty jokes or of joining the complaining crowd. We don't act as we should for fear of being rejected because of our identification with Christ, but as we do that, we have rejected Christ and his will to work in our lives. The latter is the greater of sins.

Live in the realm of the Lord's presence in your life. If you continually focus on him and what he has been doing in your life, your perspective about life, others and what they think will be changed.

Mount of Transfiguration (Mark 9:2-9)

Jesus leaves the crowd of people and takes three disciples with him up onto a high mountain. While on the mount, he is transfigured into his glorified state as John would again see him on the Isle of Patmos. As the disciple see Jesus changed and also the presence of Moses and Elijah, they become exceedingly afraid. In response to the fear, Peter suggests making three tabernacles. Peter is corrected by another manifestation of God as his voice is heard from the cloud.

Over the years, I have asked myself countless times why would Peter suggest making three tabernacles similar to that made by Moses. It is difficult to explain why we do what we do when we are afraid, but fear is Peter's reason. Man's motivation since the fall has been to perform some work in response to his fear of God. It started in the garden and has been ever present even up to today. What Peter failed to grasp is that God wanted to do a work in Peter and the others and was not looking for them to do any work.

When God reveals himself to you it is intended to affect your relationship with him and not cause you to perform a work. When he revealed himself to you at salvation, he was working to get you to cease from works and to trust him and his resurrection power for salvation. As we walk through difficult trials, we are always put into a position so that our works cannot deliver us. At some point in the trial, God will reveal himself to you. it will not be a physical manifestation, but he will reveal himself through his word. It is only when we trust him who is invisible (Heb. 11:27) that deliverance comes.

As God reveals himself to you focus on your relationship with him. Search your heart for motives, fears, selfishness, shame, goals and worries. God is trying to work on the condition of your heart. If there is a work he wants you to do, he will perform it through you when your heart is as he desires. God is concerned about what you are and not what you do for him. When you are what he wants you to be, you can then do what he wants you to do.

Law Versus Grace (Mark 10:3-4)

The Pharisees were again trying to test The Lord by posing a question that they believed to be settled by the law. Can a man divorce his wife? As The Lord answered the question, he revealed the root cause for the giving of the law: it was because of the condition of man's heart.

As you look at the law, you will see countless "thou shalts" and "thou shalt nots". The lost see these as rules for earning salvation, but as the scripture states, the law was our school master teaching us our condition before God so that we may recognize our need for a savior. Another purpose for the law was to restrict the man who walks in his flesh and to create a cognitive reminder as to limits he must live within.

However grace is just the opposite. Grace does not hinder the believer from performing any act, but is intended to enable him to perform works beyond his ability. The Pharisees, like many of us today, wanted to live their lives in the realm of the Law with the end result being a strict, stifled, unfulfilling life. However those, who have experienced victory and the abundant life, found that grace is essential for that life.

For us, we must decide how we shall conduct our lives before God. Shall we have the view of him as unaccepting and always needing to be pleased or shall we see God as our loving and accepting Father who wants to deliver us from the works of our flesh and cause us to abound in his grace. You cannot have both. Both views are manners by which believers strive to yield themselves as instruments of righteousness to God (Romans 6:13): the former unto greater bondage and the latter to victory.

One Way or the Other (Mark 10:24)

Trust is an important word in Christianity. It is similar to the word faith in that it carries the idea of being convinced or persuaded. Man's heart is the aspect of his being that contains trust. Just as you are only able to think of one thing at a time, so your heart can only focus trust on one entity at a time. The greatest problem that man has is recognizing his heart and what it is trusting.

In this passage we see a perfect example of one who believes that his life is pleasing to The Lord. He questions as to what he needs to do so that he may inherit eternal life. Jesus responded with the measuring stick of the Law. The young man, as looking into the law, saw himself as blameless. He may have appeared blameless on the outside, but his heart was a different matter. The one thing that the young man lacked was not another action, but a heart that trusted the LORD and not the idol of financial security. After his short discourse with the Lord, he is left standing at the crossroads: shall I give up everything and completely trust this Jesus or shall I hold on to what I have. His answer revealed his heart.

Before I jump on the band wagon and attack this man, I need to ask myself the following questions. How often have I balked on The Lord? Since saving my soul, how often has my heart been divided against him? How often have I been motivated by my idolatrous heart and tried to work myself out of my troubles? How often have I focused my deliverance on a person instead of The Lord? Am I trusting my job as security or am I really focusing on God? To be honest, my heart is a constant battleground. It is not so much over whom I will trust, but recognizing when my heart has turned to trusting another. The heart is still deceitful above all things and desperately wicked (Jer. 17:9).

The way to victory is to stay close to The Lord, expose yourself to his word, daily submit yourself to his will and pray for him to reveal to you the unpleasing things in your heart

Let the words of my mouth, and the meditation of my heart, be acceptable in thy sight, O Lord, my strength, and my redeemer. Psalm 19:14

5 STRENGTH FROM THE GOSPELS (PART 2)

Expectation (Mark 11:2-6)

Jesus sent his disciples into a village to get a colt. Under normal circumstances if a person were to walk up to an animal, unloose it and begin to leave, it would be considered stealing. Normal reactions would be to contact the law and prosecute. However as the owner sees these men, he ask about their intentions. Their reply of, "The Lord hath need of him" caused the owner to allow them to take his possession.

I have often thought about this passage. What took place behind the scenes? Did God previously speak to the man and let him know that the disciples of The Lord would come for the animal? Had the man recently yielded himself to the Lord and dedicated all of his possessions or did he beckon The Lord to use him in some way to bring him glory? For now, we cannot know, but what we do know is that The Lord knew how he would respond.

As I consider this text, I ask myself, " What choices does the Lord know that I will make? Is he expecting me to make choices that reflect my dedication to him or is he knowing that I will stagger in my faith? How can I know that my choices and actions will be pleasing to him? I can better accomplish this and direct my actions of the future to be pleasing to him by following a few guidelines: keep a short account of sins and confess them immediately, spend time with God in his word and in prayer, yield myself to him daily, express thanks for what he has done for me, and forgive those that have offended me. By doing these, I am not guaranteeing that all my actions will always be pleasing to him, but it will cut off those things in the world which may negatively affect me.

Sacred (Mark 11:15-17)

There are some things that God sees as sacred. Sacred is something that is set apart as holy unto God. The tabernacle was sacred as well as all of the items inside. Samson because of his Nazarite vow was sacred. The silver, gold, brass and iron of Jericho was consecrated or considered holy unto The Lord. In this passage, it was the temple. When The Lord arrived, it appeared that it was being used for every reason other than for what it was intended. There may have been offerings there, but the actions were mechanical and heartless. Greed, profit and the mundane ceremonial practices filled the place that was intended for heart communion with God.

There isn't any temple today and sacrifices are no longer needed. So what is there that is holy to God. As the temple and all other sanctified objects of the Old Testament were set apart unto The Lord, he wants our hearts set apart for him. He wants our hearts to long for his presence and to occupy themselves with motives and desires that are holy. The Lord admonishes us to keep his commandments (John 14:15). The word keep in this passages carries the idea of guarding something. The Lord wants us to guard our hearts so that only that which is pleasing to him will reside in it. The Psalmist stated it this way, "Let the words of my mouth, and the meditation of my heart, be acceptable in thy sight, O LORD, my strength, and my redeemer". (Psalm 19:14)

We cannot accomplish this task on our own, but with the power of his spirit and the working of his grace, we can have a heart like this. As you walk through life today, continually ask for God's grace to reveal that which you should shun and to direct your focus towards things that will motivate you to praise him. We don't have much to give back to him, but we do have a heart and all of its desires that can be presented to him daily.

Keeping From Error (Mark 12:24)

As the unbelievers came to Jesus to tempt him, he identified their cause of error being in that they did not know the scriptures and failed to recognize the power of God. For these people, they failed to understand marriage and also how the scriptures support that God resurrects people from the dead. Had they known truth and believed in their hearts, they would not have walked in error.

Life is not any different today. Identifying truth for life's situations and recognizing the power of God will keep you from being led astray. In order for this to happen, You must know truth that is pertinent to your life and then by faith walk believing that God will bless it and provide his powerful guidance and blessing. If you fail to seek truth for your life, you will rely upon the reasoning of your heart and that reasoning will lead you to error. There is a way which seemeth right unto a man, but the end thereof are the ways of death. (Prov. 14:12)

God reminds us that the word of God is a lamp to our feet and a light for our path. (Psalm 119:105). He will guide us to truth that will provide the direction we must go. He will not illuminate the entire way, but he will show the next step. Our part then is to believe and follow.

But if from thence thou shalt seek the Lord thy God, thou shalt find him, if thou seek him with all thy heart and with all thy soul. (Deut. 4:29)

Widows Mites (Mark 12:41-44)

In the temple was a treasury where people would give offerings to God. The rich gave from their overflow. The widow, in spite of being financially short, gave anyway. From the text, it appears that she emptied her purse. Because of her poverty, she probably did not have any savings and after her offering was given, she was without any money and needed to trust The Lord and live by faith for her next meal and supply. Why did she give? Others were giving more. Why give in this manner when the amount given would not be recognized or make any significant difference? With all the wealth given, how much of a difference would her little bit make?

Because the Lord commends her giving, her motive for providing such an offering could only have come from right motives. Truly spiritual motives for giving are empathy, obedience and love. Had the offering been used for the poor, then it would be reasonable to think that her motivation could have been from empathy, but the gifts were to be used for various purposes including servicing the temple and not just caring for the poor.

Obedience could possibly have been the motive, but most likely was not the case. In Luke 17:7-10, Jesus teaches that servants are not commended for tasks that they complete in obedience to commands of their masters. Therefore, the reasonable explanation for the widow giving so sacrificially to the point of dependency upon The Lord for her own needs to be met, could only have been motivated by love.

Love: the sacrificial desire to meet the needs of those loved. This definition describes the widow. The great question to ask is, does this definition describe you? Ask yourself, "Why do I do the things I do? Is it out of responsibility or love? Is it for what I can get back or is it from love? Is it because of who is watching or is it love? Is it because of fear or is it love?"

Christ demonstrated the greatest act of love by becoming our sin bearer. He sacrificed for what we needed. We must do the same. We must live as he lived, love as he has loved and die to self or our own desires. In doing so, we become a living testimony of his work of love in our lives.

Opportunity (Mark 13:3-9)

Opportunity: the very word reminds me of the commercial advertising the resale of football tickets. When they become available, they are only there for a moment. If you don't snatch and grab them, they will be gone.

This woman saw an opportunity, reached out and grabbed the moment. Because of it, we all have heard her testimony. However taking advantage of the opportunity was not an easy task and never really is. In this case, the woman needed to overcome personal opposition. The fact that her hair was down and she was referred to as a woman, who was a sinner, indicated that she was not accepted in the company. However, this barrier did not stop her from taking advantage of the opportunity that The Lord put upon her heart.

Opportunities come from The Lord and we must recognize and take advantage of them so that we may accomplish the work that he wants. For this woman, she had the opportunity to anoint his body for his burial. This opportunity was brought just to her. The women, who went to the tomb on resurrection morning, loved The Lord greatly, but did not have that opportunity. It was too late, he was already risen.

As I pondered this passage, I knew that I could not have the opportunities as those who were present when The Lord was on the Earth. However, I did ask myself, "What types of opportunities does The Lord bring to me?"

The Lord brings me opportunity to fellowship, serve, testify and give to him. Because I am such a fast paced person, I have probably missed out on more opportunities to fellowship with God than any other opportunities. I have needed to learn that there are sights, sounds, people and events that he brings to me daily so that I may stop, recognize his greatness and fellowship with him in praise.

Serving others is serving The Lord. He said that if a person is to be great, he will be a servant. Testifying is telling others what God has done and is doing in your life. It can be done as a response to a question from a friend or a long discussion about salvation. Giving is simply accomplished by giving yourself. After you have given yourself, giving anything else is much easier.

Today, The Lord will bring one or many opportunities your way. Will you miss the opportunity or will you snatch a grab it?

Grounded Faith (Luke 1:8-14)

The Scriptures are filled with the examples of people who lived and overcame by faith. Zacharias was one of those individuals. He and his wife were well stricken in years and yet still childless. As he served in the temple one day, he received a visit from a messenger from The Lord announcing that he and his wife would have a son. In their old age they would be blessed both physically and emotionally.

As many read this and other accounts, they see these individuals as extraordinary people with endowments upon them that we do not have, but that view is incorrect. Like us, they battled through life by faith. They may have made decisions that we fail to choose, but their lives were no different than ours. However in this account, we can see some details about Zacharias and his faith that caused him to experience victory.

Zacharias' faith endured because his life was not tainted with sin and even when he did sin, he dealt with it according to the scriptures (vs. 6). As he lived a life of faith, he chose to pray in the face of adverse circumstances and believed that God could work and give him a child regardless of what the circumstances conveyed (vs. 13). How long he prayed is not known, but while he waited, he continued to serve The Lord (vs. 8-9). Then when he least expected it, his faith took him to the answer and promise as presented by the angel.

Remember as you prayerfully face your trials of circumstances which appear insurmountable, keep yourself from sin and when you fall deal with it as God has instructed, believe that God can overcome your circumstances and faithfully serve him while you wait for his answer.

Seeking For Jesus (Luke 2:49)

This passage is very familiar because it is the first recording of words spoken by Jesus. His statement, "How is it that ye sought me? wist ye not that I must be about my Father's business?" is made in reply to his mother who in exasperation from searching for him questioned his behavior. In today's terms he would be telling her that she really didn't need to search for him because she should know where he would be: going about his father's business.

Jesus has promised to never leave or forsake us, but we can stray or wander away from him. The question is, "Can we ever really lose Jesus to where we need to search for him so that we can get back?" If we were to ask The Lord, his answer would be very similar to the reply made to his mother. He would probably tell us, "You don't need to search for me. You will find me where you left me."

When people stray from The Lord, it is usually around an event or circumstance. It may result from being hurt in losing a loved one. It could have resulted from a sickness in themselves or someone that they love greatly. They may have strayed because they ran after an empty opportunity offered by the world or their trust in others may have been shattered. In any event, people usually stray in response to life and its circumstances.

How do these people get back? The answer: they need to return to where they left The Lord. If they accused him of not caring, then they need to return to him, confess their error and exercise faith that God does care. If they were lured by the trinkets of the world, they need to return, confess loving another and set their affection on things above. If they felt abandoned, they need to cease believing that lie and instead tell God that they will believe the promises of his word. When a person is away from God, they strongly believe the lies of the enemy just as much as we believe the promises of God and the only answer is repentance. That is to change their mind from what they believe or think to something different. Abraham experienced this when he went back to Bethel. It was there that he built an altar and met with God and it was there that he returned to God after coming out of Egypt.

This is a very difficult thing to accomplish and the longer somebody is away from The Lord the more difficult the task will be. However with God nothing shall be impossible. If you have wandered away, come back to God. You will find him at your Bethel. If you have a son, daughter or loved one who has wandered away, continue praying for them. God wants them to come back to him much more than you do.

Our Enemy (Luke 4:2-14)

After Jesus' baptism, the spirit of God led Jesus into the wilderness. While there, he was tempted by the devil who used all of his power and expected him to fall as every person before who had been tempted had fallen. The power displayed by the devil is only a portion of his potential and reveals to us that our tempter is not on an equal plane with us.

The devil had the power to take Jesus to a high mountain and reveal to him all kingdoms of the Earth. Regardless of how high a mountain, there was no way that all kingdoms could be viewed naturally. Satan made this possible with the power that he had given to him at his creation. He then took him from the wilderness to a high pinnacle of the temple. Who would allow them access to this holy place and how would they get to the high pinnacle? The temple was not a multistoried building. Again, the devil used his power to make this possible. Other passages reveal that he is a deceiver (1 Timothy 2:14), the father of lies (John 8:44), and can make himself appear as an angel of light (2 Cor. 11:14).

From Jesus' temptation and this information, you can formulate a strategy of defense. To be victorious, you must recognize that your enemy, as he displayed in his tempting of Jesus, has greater power than you and you cannot defeat him in your own strength. Just as you needed Jesus to deliver you from the penalty and bondage of sin, you need him to deliver you from the temptation to sin. You also must recognize that the enemy will make promises that he cannot or will not keep. Although his promises may appear to be pleasing, sin always robs the believer of the joy they are seeking. It is also important for the believer to settle the matter in their heart that supernatural happenings should not be immediately credited to God. The way to be cautious is to make sure that actions believed to be from God do not contradict God's word. God is not the author of confusion. Therefore, he will not say one thing in his word and then do another.

God has promised to guide, direct, comfort and empower us. With these promises of his presence, power, and directing, we cannot fail.

<u>Worthy-Unworthy (Luke 7:2-10)</u>

Why do some people experience miraculous works of God in their lives and others do not? Why can some pray and receive from God and others miss that experience? The passage of the centurion reveals some qualities necessary for such to occur.

Before a miracle (an act that is the result of God's direct intervention) can occur, there must be a need. We have been in situations like this many times in our lives involving financial, health, domestic and safety needs.

What also is necessary is that there needs to be an absence of pride. The centurion sees himself as unworthy, which is contrary to how others viewed him. His view was not one of self rejection, pity or false humility, but a view that he fell short of meeting the mark for being worthy to face and ask Jesus for help. Because we are in Christ and the Holy Spirit is in us, we should never see ourselves as unworthy with coming to Christ because Hebrews 4:16 tells us to come boldly to the throne of grace. However, pride can take many forms. It can be displayed by us resisting God and refusing to seek his help or it can cloak itself by praying to God for help and then beginning to try working out deliverance on its own.

The final quality needed is faith. Jesus recognized the centurion for his faith as demonstrated by his statement that Jesus only needed to speak the word and his servant would be healed. We too must walk in similar faith believing that God is able to deliver us from our plight and then just rest in him. Remember when you came to Christ for salvation, you were in a struggle between working for salvation and trusting him. When you finally settled the matter in your heart, refused to pridefully work for salvation and then called upon Jesus as Savior, you rested in the finished work of Christ on the cross. No longer did you labor for acceptance with God, but rested in him and believed that you were accepted in the beloved. This rest can and should be experienced by believers beyond their call for salvation. God wants you to experience his rest as he continually delivers you from trials and struggles.

The Pruning Process (Luke 8:15)

It is now rolling towards my favorite time of year. Soon, I will be planting tomatoes, peppers, and various herbs. But as I sit on my patio, I am looking at my fig tree. Last year was the first year that I planted it. During the winter months, I pruned the branches so that it would produce an abundance of fruit this year. Pruning causes plants to grow more shoots, which will produce more fruit.

It is the same with believers. This parable indicates that those who will produce an abundance of fruit in their lives are those who have the right heart condition, hear the word of God and hold onto it, and do so with patience. The word used for patience has been defined as remaining under.

The Lord says that he is the vine and we are the branches and that he purges or prunes branches so that they may bring forth more fruit. When does this pruning take place and what does it look like? Is it accomplished by The Lord cutting away sin from our lives? That would not be a bad idea, but it is not the case. Is it accomplished by the Lord removing people from our lives who may cause us to stumble? Again, not a bad idea but not the case.

Pruning is accomplished by the situations brought into our lives that we are forced to face with patience. The Lord stated that those who bear under will be producing fruit. We bear under when we live under trials and endure them by faith. When we refuse to remain in the trials brought to us or allowed by The Lord, the pruning process stops. He does not cut away the branches of our vine in moments of time. Instead he is removing that which hinders us from producing by allowing those great trials that we face and dread. They are our refining fires and also our pruning hooks.

As you face your trials today, don't look at them as the dreaded portion of your life, but instead the opportunity to remove that which hinders you the most.

God's Power Flowing In Our Lives (Luke 8:46)

As I took another look at the passage of the woman with this issue of blood, I could not help but focus on the Lord knowing he was touched for healing because he felt virtue or his power go out from him. Many others who touched up against him did not experience his power nor did his power flow out from him, but only this woman. The reason was because by faith she was looking to him for the help that she thought and believed only he could give.

We can experience this same power today because when we reach out in faith to God, it releases his power into our lives. In my daily living, I continually need God's power to flow into my life or better said flow out of my life. I am thankful that his spirit lives within me. Because of him, I already possess the same power that flowed into that woman on that miraculous day.

All I need for this to happen is to believe, pray and trust. Easier said than done, right? In order to believe, I must fight the battle in my mind against the lies that my flesh and the enemy bring.

(For the weapons of our warfare are not carnal, but mighty through God to the pulling down of strong holds;) Casting down imaginations, and every high thing that exalteth itself against the knowledge of God, and bringing into captivity every thought to the obedience of Christ; (2 Cor. 10:4-5)

As our heart experiences the victory over the doubts created by these lies, we are then moved to pray. Prayer before this point was only hopeful words aimed at convincing God to work, but with faith and truth, prayer is changed into something powerful. After interacting with God through faith, we can then decide to rest in him, his power and promises.

Are you resting in him? If not, it's not a matter of praying harder, but instead praying with faith in light of his truth.

Alone In The Trial (Luke 8:43-48)

Trials are difficult times for everyone. What may seem to be the greatest difficulty with trials is that when you are in them, you feel all alone. You may be surrounded by friends and family, but in the midst of the crowd, you stand alone. The reason you feel alone is because nobody is experiencing the array of emotions that flood your heart. These people may want to help, but all their efforts may come up empty because they are not in touch with what is happening in your heart.

This is the case for the woman with the issue of blood. Because of Levitical guidelines, she was considered unclean. Being separated from society and treated as an outcast probably brought more hurt and pain than her medical condition. From the scriptural account, we see that nobody was able to help and many probably could have cared less. What probably brought her help and hope were the testimonies that she heard from others.

The problem of people feeling alone in their trials continues to occur today. What causes greater pain for them is when others, with whom they fellowship in Christ, look at them in judgment. As Job had friends who accused him of not being spiritual, fellow believers do the same by their words, their avoidance or how they gaze at those in trials.

However, that is not what The Lord intended. By his sovereignty, he leads us into and through trials so that as he being touched with the feeling of our infirmities made himable to minister into us (Hebrews 4:14-15), we can do the same for others. II Corinthians 1 says that as Christ has comforted us in our tribulation, we may be able to comfort others in the same manner as we were comforted.

God never intended for us to be alone or feel alone. He has promised to never leave us or forsake us. He has also provided others to give us empathy and comfort as he has provided to them. However as great as this is, many fail to receive the compassion and encouragement that they need. This happens because we fail others even though Christ has not failed us.

The Error of Martha (Luke 10:38-42)

Mary and Martha were sisters with two different types of relationships with The Lord. This passage tells us that Jesus had been invited to their home and the sisters had different responses to him being in the house. The two relationships are displayed in that Mary was focused on Jesus and getting closer to him and Martha was concerned with serving.

Service is an important part of the Christian life, but it should not be the focal point. Our focus should always be on our relationship with The Lord. By doing so, we will be closer to him and more sensitive to his voice. However living a life that is focused on serving The Lord will bring with it a series of problems and create conditions in the heart.

When you live a life focused on service, your life becomes cumbersome or you get distracted with being busy and striving for results. This need for success or results creates the same anxiety and crowding in that Martha experienced. It is at this point that you will fall as Martha did to having a wrong view of The Lord and begin questioning his concern for you and the work you are doing. You, as Martha did, will develop a victim complex in service causing you to focus on what others are not doing and become bothered with them. Eventually the saddest of traits will be developed in the heart when God becomes your tool or servant for accomplishing the tasks. Martha demonstrated this by telling The Lord to address the issue with her sister's lack of support and help.

However if we were to be as Mary and focus on The Lord and the relationship that he wants to have with us, we will not fall privy to the pitfalls as did Martha. Works of service will not be for the reaching of goals or the establishment of success, but out of a heart of love and devotion. As Paul stated that the greatest of gifts is love: it is still true today.

Make sure as you serve, you don't serve service, but serve The Lord.

Serve the Lord with gladness: ... Psalm 100:2

Being a Disciple (Luke 14:33-34)

When my daughter was a little girl, she had a favorite stuffed animal. Wherever she went, it was always with her. When she was admitted to the hospital as an infant, we left it at home thinking that the hospital would not permit it there. Needless to say, another stuffed animal needed to be purchased. Her little stuffed bunny stayed with her in the hospital and everywhere that she went. She slept, played and ate with bunny. Needless to say, when it was time for bunny to move on, she was not pleased and wanted to hold on to it regardless of its condition.

As adults we sometimes function in the same manner. We hold onto things thinking they will help us be what we want to be, but they really keep us from being what we could be. There are supposed securities in our lives that we cling to and we keep these to help us face our fears in life. These securities may be people, vocations, savings, alcohol and medication or walls of protection that we put up to keep people and things from hurting us.

People are not God and will always come up short when it comes to protecting you or meeting your needs. As we saw a few years with the financial structure of the United States, the bottom can fall out at any time and the effects can be devastating. Finances are never a security and are nothing more than a house of cards. When times of stress crowd people in, some believers turn to alcohol or drugs. By these tools, they adjust their moods and either remove the stress or gain the courage to move forward. In the past, great walls protected cities from attack. In like manner, people build walls in their lives to protect them from people and life events. Whenever they face trials or oppositions, they retreat behind their walls and protect themselves.

These and other qualities are the very things that God wants us to forsake so that we can be a disciple of Christ. Our success in Christ is not solely caused by what we do or the qualities that we may have, but is more so based on how little baggage we are carrying. What hinders believers the most is a double heart meaning a heart for Christ our fortress and one that also is holding on to other securities.

What is hindering you from being a disciple? What in your life are you trusting instead of Christ or in addition to Christ? In spite of it, the Lord has brought you this far. Now is the time, to let it go.

Compassion (Luke 15:20)

The story of the prodigal son is familiar to most people. It has been preached countless times and expounded upon in many ways. Most focus on the passage in light of a salvation account, but the purpose of the parable was in response to the Scribes and Pharisees' accusation of Jesus receiving sinners (vs. 2). It is another story revealing the compassionate heart of God towards sinners who come to him. From the qualities displayed by the father in the parable, we can measure our heart for compassion towards those that God loves.

While the son was off at a distant land wasting his life, the father did not go after him and try to deliver him from the circumstances in life that the son brought upon himself. If we have compassion, we will not enable other people in their sin by trying to remove their consequences to protect us from shame or embarrassment. By doing this, we, with compassion, are more concerned about them than ourselves.

Compassion will cause you to desire the fallen to come back to the Lord. It is my belief that the father saw the son a great way off because he continually desired and looked for the day that he would return. When we have compassion, we will see people who are far away from The Lord and our hearts will be moved with the desire that they would return. When the son returned, he was not questioned by the father about where he had been and what he had done. He was received with gladness. When sinners return, we too out of compassion will leap at the opportunity to receive them without asking questions (vs. 20).

As a musician is compelled to play music because of what is inside of him, compassionate people cannot hold back compassion, but must show it. They, from compassion, will celebrate the victories of the restored (vs. 20) and bring others into the rejoicing (vs. 22-23). From there, they will invite them back into fellowship and will lead others to do the same.

They accomplish all this by one means: they focus on the person and not the sin. This quality is missing in so many circles of our faith. Compassion is the manifestation of love that Jesus said would be the means by which all men shall know that we are his disciples. What do the lost need from us? Compassion. What do people in the church need from us? Compassion. What do you and I need from others? Compassion.

Finally, be ye all of one mind, having compassion one of another, love as brethren, be pitiful, be courteous: (1Peter 3:8)

Offenses (Luke 17:1-5)

It is impossible but that offences will come: but woe unto him, through whom they come!

This passage admonishes us about offenses and warns us that what is worse than an offense is to be the person bringing it. With the words "take heed", he begins to discuss forgiving those who have wronged us that repented and are seeking forgiveness. What this passage teaches is that people who bring offenses are those which will not forgive others who wronged them.

Each of us sin daily and the sins that we commit affect those around us. People may not see or experience the direct results of each committed sin, but as we live out of fellowship with God and walk in our flesh, the actions that we commit during that time do affect those around us. Our short fuse, uncooperative spirit, complaining, etc. wounds others and we are wounded by the same in them. Because of this, we will need to forgive or seek forgiveness from others.

However, when we refuse to forgive and restore fellowship with brothers or sisters in Christ, we commit an occasion against them that is an offense, snare or occasion to fall. This behavior is contrary to biblical teaching and is warned against by The Lord. It hinders the growth and spiritual condition of both involved: the repentant is hindered from complete restoration and may continue to carry guilt and the unforgiving will fail in experiencing forgiveness and avoiding temptation (Matt. 6:12-13).

When we refuse to forgive, we attempt to exact our judgment upon the person who sinned against us or to bring them to a point of performing some action to demonstrate their degree of sorrow and repentance for their sin. This sin of not forgiving is not their greatest. Their greatest sin is living in the place of God and through their own decision making decides who should be forgiven and by what criteria needs to be met before forgiveness is to be granted. Because of this condition, The Lord brings a warning of woe to such believers.

We have been forgiven of a great debt. When The Lord forgave us, he made a right decision that met his criteria and then performed a wonderful work in us. We as believers need to allow God that same opportunity with others. By not forgiving, we hinder God, the repentant and also bring a woe upon ourselves.

Worthless (Luke 18:1)

When growing up, I lived in the Italian immigrant section of town. Although it had been established some 60 years earlier, it continued to reflect the culture of the people group. One such practice was the inserting of Italian words into the English conversation. Many times when something was considered worthless the word kaka was used. This word carried various meanings from dirt on the hands to human or animal excrement. A word similar to this is used in this passage.

We are exhorted that we should pray and not faint. The two words are contrasts or opposite ends of the spectrum. When we pray, we are communicating or pointing the desires or needs of our hearts toward God. In fact, it is the fulfillment of casting our cares on him as instructed in 1 Peter 5:7. When we faint, when have turned and headed in a worthless direction*.

This is the fulcrum or pivotal point of the Christian life. Our success has never hinged or been determined by our performance, knowledge, dedication, or past performance. It has and will always be based on the condition of the heart and the battle that takes place there. In trials, your heart will either reflect on God and his promises and then turn to him or it will turn in the opposite direction towards worthless or bad responses.

This is the battleground. This is where people make it or are broken. However, this also is where God wants to meet with you, help you and provide to you much needed strength. So as you endure another trial of your faith, feed your heart with the word of God which produces faith, resists thoughts that come from your flesh and the enemy and pour out your heart to him.

* ek kakos: from a point moving to bad or worthless

Praying To Get (Luke 19:37-38)

Jesus was entering Jerusalem. As he rode, the people were casting palms and clothes before him. Their hearts were rejoicing and their mouths extended words of praise. At first glance, it seemed as if they were accepting him, but they were not. They were accepting a person whom they believed would give them what they wanted, but instead, Jesus was bringing to them what they needed. After being beaten and scourged, it was apparent that their hopes of an earthly king were dashed. When it was believed that he could not fulfill their expectations, they rejected him. Many who read this account judge the Jews as foolish for rejecting him. However before being quick to judge, you may want to search your own heart for similar motives.

How often are your prayers focused on what you want God to do for you? How often do you pray for a need to be met or an undesirable situation be removed? Do your prayers continually focus on relief from hurt, pain, trouble or fear? If so, you may have more in common with those in Jerusalem than you thought.

God did not save us so that we could have him at our disposal, but instead redeemed us so that we may be at his. It is not wrong to pour out your heart to God and ask for deliverance. Jesus did the very thing in the garden of Gethsemane, but along with that he coupled his heart's request with submission to his father's divine plan. If you have been praying for the same trial to be removed or for circumstances in life to change, why not change your request and ask for strength to endure, power in living for a testimony to others or for the trial to prune away that from your life, which hinders you from producing fruit for him.

If you make this change, God will hear and answer. However if you continue praying in your same manner, you may become discouraged and possibly turn your heart against him in the same way as those in Jerusalem did. Over the years, I have met countless people who have become angry with God and the similar thread is that they prayed and God did not deliver as expected. God wants to deliver, but he will do it in his time and manner. He may deliver you from the trial or he may deliver you through the trial. Until then, make sure that the requests of your prayers align with his will. The answer is not praying more or harder, but instead to submit yourself to his will and abide in him.

John 15:7 If ye abide in me, and my words abide in you, ye shall ask what ye will, and it shall be done unto you.

Rejected For His Name's Sake (Luke 21:17)

And ye shall be hated of all men for my name's sake. Luke 21:17

Do you find yourself cut off from others. Do others act together in friendship in and outside of the work environment, but exclude you? Do you experience attitudes of rejection without identifying what you could have done to bring it upon you? The good news is that you are not alone and it is not just your imagination. The cause of the rejection is probably your testimony of faith.

There are some people who are rejected because they take or make opportunity to give the gospel whether the individuals wants to hear it or not. They may be rejected because of their faith or possibly not and just because of their demeanor. Sometimes people like this bring rejection upon themselves. Sometimes their actions are right meaning they are led of God and other times their actions are not right because they are motivated by self or selfish reasons.

There are others who reach out to workers in love and try to be a help and support. They strive to be a friend and build relationships with others so as to be a source of help for them in times of crisis. As loving as these people can be, they still find themselves rejected. The reason this occurs is because of their testimony for God and righteousness. Each time the lost see them, they are reminded of the error of their ways. Regardless of their humanistic views, they still become convicted by the Holy Spirit and the conviction often times comes when they see you.

I remember one occasion when I took a position as an electrician at a small manufacturing plant. News ran through the building about a new employee coming who was a ministry major in college. On the day that I walked in the door, I had more than half of the employees refuse to speak to me or even say hello. I didn't even have the opportunity to do anything to make them made at me. Why was I treated in such a fashion? They hated me because of his name's sake.

As you struggle through life and the trials that it brings along with experiencing this same rejection, do not be discouraged. They are not rejecting you, they are rejecting Christ. This thought does not take away the hurt of rejection, but it should keep you from thinking it is for personal reasons.

Intercede For Others (Luke 22:32)

But I have prayed for thee, that thy faith fail not: and when thou art converted, strengthen thy brethren. Luke 22:32

Peter was determined that he would be faithful to The Lord: even unto death. But regardless of his intentions, he still fell and did so terribly. In our own lives, we have been close to The Lord and believed that because of what we have experienced in him, we would never fail or falter. However to our dismay, we have found ourselves fallen to the wiles of the enemy who also desired to sift us like wheat.

Thanks be to God that even though we may fall, God's plan for us is not over. He did not condone our actions which led us to fall away or into sin, but he has determined that he would use these occasions to strengthen us and make us a help and influence on others. A just man may fall seven times, but he always gets up again and we are promised that it is the Lord's grace that is picking us up and that he will be there waiting to help and restore us.

This work of conversion or turning around is accomplished by God, but is dependent on the prayers of others. We have a responsibility to brothers and sisters in the faith to pray for them regardless of how badly they have fallen and to carrying them in our hearts before God so that they may be restored. Many times our prayers for the fallen have selfish motives. We may want them to turn so that they no longer bring shame to the church or the family. Their turning may make our lives more at ease or we may pray because we need them back in a ministry, a number to be counted or another person to offer tithes and offerings.

Jesus interceded for Peter. In other words, he prayed for the benefit of Peter and what Peter would need. Our prayers for others are greatly needed, but the prayers must be for others and not for something to be done in their lives for our benefit. This is true intercessory prayer.

Pray and Submit (Luke 22:41-42)

Prayer is an important part of the Christian's life. There are many promises concerning prayer. We are told that if we ask, we shall receive. So that the Father may be glorified in the Son, we can ask in Jesus' name and receive it. To those who abide in the vine, asking what they will shall be granted. But what do you do when you are struggling in a trial? You don't feel as if you are abiding because the world is turned up side down. You are so confused and you can't tell what is God's will. You are afraid that if you ask for something in particular, God may become angry with your request. So then, how do you with great confidence pray?

From Jesus' prayer in the garden, we learn that it is okay to simply pour out your heart and ask God for what you want. It may sound selfish, but it is alright. You may pray that God would take vengeance on your enemies or on those that are trying to destroy you. David did so with great liberty. You may be asking for monetary gain, healing or some other form of divine intervention. However, after bearing your burden to God and asking for what you want, you should submit yourself to him and his divine plan. That is what Jesus did. He actually asked that if possible, the cross could be avoided, but then submitted to the Father's will. I am really glad for the submitting. Had it not been for those few words, I would still be lost and continue to experience all the hurt that came along with it.

So, when you are in a trial, pray for your heart's desire, but don't forget to submit to God and his plan. As we benefited from Christ's submission, somebody needs your submission as well.

Praying for Strength (Luke 22:44)

And being in an agony he prayed more earnestly: and his sweat was as it were great drops of blood falling down to the ground. Luke 22:44

While in the garden, Jesus was in agony. At this time, he was not beaten nor had he experienced any wounds. The agony experienced by Jesus was an internal struggle that he faced. The previous verse seems to indicate that the angel strengthened or invigorated him physically. As God he could not struggle spiritually. Therefore, the internal struggle must have been an emotional one.

How did he seek or gain emotional strength? He gained it by praying more earnestly. As we seek God's face and pray, we gain strength in the area that we become the most weak. As we struggle emotionally through trials, don't forget that God wants to strength you so that you can stand and bear the emotions of your trial. Remember, prayer is not just a time for communicating with God, but an opportunity to gain what is needed for victory in the emotional struggle that accompanies trials.

Father Forgive Them (Luke 23:34)

Why did Jesus say, "Father forgive them, for they know not what they do". Didn't the father know that they did not know what they were doing? Was not the father willing to forgive? Why was the son willing to forgive and the father not?

God, The Father, has many attributes, but his governing attribute is holiness. All his actions stem from demonstrating holiness or satisfying it. He is the Judge of all the Earth and has demonstrated this by his actions towards the kingdoms of the Earth.

From Jesus' birth until his return to Earth for setting up his kingdom, he personifies mercy and truth. All that he did was to fulfill him seeking and saving that which was lost. The attributes we saw him demonstrate on Earth are the same qualities that he has as our High Priest. The problem we have is that we view him in our relationship as a holy and righteous judge, when he continues to deal with us in meekness, kindness and love. Yes, he continues to hate sin, but he is concerned about helping, healing and empowering us for victory.

With the exception of his dealing with the hypocritical Pharisees, he always dealt with fallen sinners in love and mercy. We must remember that he reaches out to us in this same manner. We no longer need not walk before him in fear. He is there to help, there to pick you up, there to restore you and will do all this in love. What a wonderful savior!

6 STRENGTH FROM OTHER PASSAGES

<u>Plucked Out (Galatians 1:4)</u>

I love to garden. Each year I grow more tomato plants than my family could possibly need. In order to have the over flow of fruit, the garden needs to be weeded regularly. The easiest way to accomplish this is to use a hoe and to dig the weeds up from the ground. Instead of gathering them, they can be left on top of the dirt to be dried out by the sun. However, there have been times that before they were dried up, the weeds took root again.

This is much the same with the Christian life. When Jesus gave himself for us, he did so that he may deliver us from this present evil world. The word used for deliver can also be translated "to tear out" or "to pluck". Before trusting Christ, we were in the world and the world was in us. The world or better yet, the world system was rooted in us and we were rooted in the system. But thanks be to God, Jesus came so that he may deliver us from the power of sin and the hurt associated with it. To accomplish this, he plucked us out by the roots. However, he left us here as a testimony for him and to know him better.

While here, we must remain close to him by abiding in him and his word. This is much more than going through the act of reading and praying, but instead to be involved in worship and fellowship with God. If we fail, our hearts, as the weeds in my garden, will again begin to take root in the world. Without the sweetness of fellowshipping with him, our hearts will long for the former things. We will be tempted to look back and as many have in the past, go back.

Stay close to the Savior. Don't allow your walk with him to become routine. Share with a friend what you gain in devotions and allow them to do the same. As iron sharpens iron, your fellowship can sharpen each other for Christ (Prov. 27:17). Jesus is the best thing in your life, don't mss out on what he has to offer you.

Be Free – Live Free (Galatians 4:9)

Not long ago when you were lost, you were bound in your sin. Your sin nature controlled you just as a bound prisoner is controlled by his captors. You did not decide to sin, sin decided for you and you did as it pleased. As you continued in this state, your heart became heavy and burdensome. You longed for relief from hurt and for something better. You did not know what it was, but innately you longed for it anyway. Then God began to bring truth to you. For moments of time, your blinded eyes were opened and you began to see a hope for your state of bondage. Then on that most memorable day, truth removed the callousness of your heart and the scales from your eyes to the blinding beautiful light of the gospel and you became free. For the first time, you could live without succumbing to the dictates of your sin nature. You began to enjoy life in a way previously unimaginable and it all came about with your liberty in Christ.

The Galatians experienced the same thing, but instead of continually enjoying the liberty that they had in Christ, they allowed themselves to be brought again into bondage. They again embraced the law as a manner of completing them spiritually. How did this happen and why were they able to be led away from truth?

One key from scripture that reveals why people allow themselves to be brought again into bondage is fear (Gal. 2:12). Even Peter himself because of fear gave in and placed himself under the law. Fear of rejection, fear of failure and fear of being in error can all be motivators. People who before salvation lived under some of these afore mentioned fears are likely candidates for submitting to bondage. Another cause for bondage to occur is because a leader attempts to promote himself among those he seeks to lead into bondage or to promote himself among his own peers (Gal. 4:17).

Have you placed yourself back into bondage? Ask yourself, "What am I doing to make myself justified before God or man? What rigid code am I following to make me appear just or justified before my peers?" You may believe in eternal security and may resist law keeping in order to attain salvation, but by what standard do you measure your spirituality or by what standard do you allow others to measure you? If it is by anything other than recognizing the fruit of the spirit in your life (Gal. 5:22-23) you are in bondage. The fruit of the Holy Spirit will reveal God's holiness in your life. Paul condemns using liberty as an occasion for the flesh, but does promote godly living.

You can live free from the bondage of sin and God wants to assure that you never again come into bondage either to sin or any other entity. Decide today to be free and live free.

Loving People Back (Galatians 4:16)

Am I therefore become your enemy, because I tell you the truth? Gal. 4:16

As believers struggle through life battling the flesh, they sometimes fall privy to the attacks of the enemy. They may become misled in doctrine by wrongful influences or are overcome by hurt, fear, anxiety or sorrow. At these times, God will work to bring them back to himself. If they are reading the scriptures, he will speak to them through his word. However many times those who have fallen to the enemies' attacks fail to seek his face. They continue to be overcome and misled by the influences upon their hearts. It is then that The Lord begins to use people to bring them back to himself. He does this because in the midst of all the voices of influence upon the heart, an audible voice sounds more clearly like a trumpet sounding in the midst of the confusion of battle. The audible voice God uses may be a friend, spouse, pastor or parent.

In this same manner, Paul reaches out to the Galatians who are living in error. You would think that his apostleship alone should be enough to lead them back, but it could not. If a person is deceived to the point of resisting God, they can just as easily resist the earthly voice. You also would think that Paul reminding them of doctrinal teachings should turn them from error, but again it alone is not enough. The greatest influence

Paul has to turn the Galatians back to God is the love relationship that they have between each other. He reminds them of their love for him and presses upon them his love and concern for them. He is not attacking them so as to overcome and bring them back: he is trying to love them back.

Are there people that you know who are away from God? There are enough people in the world trying to push, shame, badger or punish them in order to get them to get right with God. Why don't you decide to be one of the few who will try to love them back. Your love will make the message of your voice be heard clearly and more apt to be received.

But speaking the truth in love... Ephesians 4:15

A Purpose for Trials (Philippians 3:10)

Trials, why do we have them? Each of us has heard countless messages on this topic and we are always attentive to the help they bring because it seems that we almost continually live our lives in the midst of trials. However, it seems that a common theme for all of the messages is that the trial is intended to develop or strengthen our faith. This is true, but trials are not only intended to develop our faith. Sometimes trials are intended to make our lives an example to the lost. God may allow a trial so that the lost may see the grace of God evident in our lives. Another purpose is so that we may be equipped to help others through their trials (2 Cor. 1). However, a purpose that is most often overlooked is for knowing or understanding Jesus.

Have you ever been in a trial or are you currently in one now where you believe that you cannot take another step or you cannot go another day? It is in this time that God wants you to learn of his dear son. Jesus too was at a point in his life where he physically could not take another step, yet he continued to take unobtainable steps to the cross. His trembling legs and body racked with pain screamed, "You cannot go any farther!" Yet he did. As you are weary, think of him and his love for you and the

Father that strengthened your steps. During this time, God wants you to learn about his son by experiencing what he experienced.

Has your trial hurt you deeply? Is your heart aching with no relief in sight? Have you been to the point where your insides draw up into a knot, your bowels stab with pain or you become sick with sorrow? Jesus has. It began in the garden and was multiplied as he hung alone on the cross. He could have stopped it all and been right for doing so. As God, he could have done as he pleased, but what pleased him most was you, me and his father. As you ache, begin to understand Jesus. It is one of the purposes for the trial. It seems that this is explained best in Philippians 3:10, "That I may know him, and the power of his resurrection, and the fellowship of his sufferings...

Many people, at these points in their trials, have given up. Because of their struggle to go further or their perceived inability to deal with the pain of the trial, they quit. They quit on God and missed out on knowing him and understanding the true depth of his love.

Forgetting Those Things Which Are Behind (Philippians 3:13-14)

This great passage has been a help to many with maintaining or gaining a right focus. However, so many people have misused this passage or applied it incorrectly to their lives or the lives of others. Probably the most damage has occurred when people, who have been wounded by abuse, have been told that they don't need to get closure or help in dealing with their wounds that have caused them to fight anger, bitterness, depression and anxiety, but instead forget about their past and those things that are behind and press forward for Jesus. I am glad to say that the meaning of this passage is something completely different.

In verse three, Paul makes an important statement. He speaks about worshipping God and rejoicing in Christ and then says, "And have no confidence in the flesh." From there, Paul boasts on everything from being circumcised on the eighth day, to persecuting the church and finally touching the righteousness of the law and being blameless. He then sums it up with counting all things but loss, accounting his righteousness because of Christ and recognizing that he has not arrived. After the contrast is made between his life in the law and now in Christ, Paul's says, "Forgetting those things which are behind, and reaching forth unto those things which are before, I press toward the mark for the prize of the high calling of God in Christ Jesus." In other words, Paul is saying that his focus is not on his past accomplishments, but instead on what he is in Christ and that he will determinately and faithfully stand and live for him.

A practical application would be to recognize that what you were will not provide the success, accountability and influence for today and tomorrow. You cannot live on past victory and success because today is another day that brings its own trials and work. Just as past success cannot determine today's victory, sins of the past are not a determination for today or future failures.

So be like Paul and forget about your past in the flesh, forget about your past spiritual accomplishments and make today count, because it is the only day that you have the power to change.

Root of Bitterness (Hebrews 12:15)

Looking diligently lest any man fail of the grace of God; lest any root of bitterness springing up trouble you, and thereby many be defiled;

Bitterness may spring up like a root, but if left unattended, will grow to mammoth proportions. Bitterness in the heart of the believer is like a poison. Important questions to ask are how does a person become bitter and where does bitterness come from?

As humans, we interact with people daily and in that interaction, we can be offended or hurt. If we carry these hurts in our hearts and fail to forgive as the scriptures instruct, the hurts will remain. As future days pass, daily hurts continue to accumulate. If this process continues for a while, it will not be long until the individual is facing major issues of hurt and anger. This person's anger will continue to grow towards others and even themselves for allowing the hurt to happen. Bitterness develops from unresolved hurt and anger. Anger is best described as a person's emotional state, but bitterness will develop and become their attitude or perspective towards life and others.

To keep yourself from being overcome with hurt, anger and bitterness, you must forgive those who have sinned or wronged you. Forgives means to release. A common phrase that people say today instead of telling people to forgive is, "Let it go". When we forgive, we let people go or release them from any obligation towards us. Because they don't owe us, it will be difficult to become angry towards them and without anger, there also be an absence of bitterness.

So, as you face people daily who hurt or offend you, look for reasons why you should forgive them. It may be because of issues in their lives. It may be because of things that you have done towards them or possibly because they simply may be having a bad day. But by releasing them, you are really freeing yourself from all of the baggage that leads to bitterness.

Take a quick inventory of your life. If you have hurt, anger or bitterness, identify the causes and those involved and LET THEM GO!

Let all bitterness, and wrath, and anger, and clamour, and evil speaking, be put away from you, with all malice: And be ye kind one to another, tenderhearted, forgiving one another, even as God for Christ's sake hath forgiven you. Ephesians 4:31-31

God's Completing Work (James 1:4)

Grin and bear it. How many times has that been said to you or you have said it to yourself? I remember a comic strip in the papers that boasted that title. It was about the trials in life that we need to just deal with and move on. There is a biblical term that has much the same meaning. It is, patience. Patience is not waiting because waiting only entails enduring until the end. However patience is enduring until the end, but with cheerfulness. How many people have you met who are in the midst of a great trial and struggle and yet they remain cheerful. It isn't any secret to have that attitude because it will result from the Holy Spirit meeting with you and changing your hopeless view to that which agrees with his perspective.

But, how do I get this view? You get this view by seeing the end. Just as God sees the end from the beginning, so you need to do the same. You may not be able to see the details as he sees them, but you can see that all things work together for good to them that love God, to them who are the called according to his purpose. You can see that whatever takes place it will be what is best for you and greatest for his glory. You can even see that God will continue to be in control and that whatever happens, is only by his will that it can take place. When you truly have this perspective, you will also have patience.

Now when you have patience, it will do a work for you and in you. When you allow God to do his complete work in your life, you become complete. The word perfect in this passage does not pertain to somebody who is without sin, wrong or error, but it means to be complete as in a complete set. Patience is what you need so that you can be what you are intended to be. The only place that You can get it is from trials. Trials bring you to the end of yourself and when You are there, it is then that God can do something in and through you.

So, think of your trial. Will you allow it to cause you to give up and quit, or will you yield to God so that he can do something even greater in your life: the completing work of patience?

The Opportunity of Trials (James 1:12-16)

In the Christian life, there are so many blessings from God. Our mates, children, jobs, health, answered prayers and abilities are just a few that can be mentioned. However, this passage identifies one blessing that most of us would not have recognized. God says that for those who experience trials and endure them, they will be blessed. The blessing is two-fold: they will be happy and they will receive a crown of life.

Trials in themselves are not events that we enjoy nor do we look forward to them. However, they are an ever present part of our lives. This passage of scripture contains truths necessary to understand for us to be victorious through trials.

When you are in a trial, it has either come from God or has been allowed by God to occur. It is intended for the purpose of putting you on display with the intent of proving something to be acceptable. You are not tried to prove to see if you should be accepted by God because positionally you are already accepted in the beloved. However, you are a vessel of mercy intended to prove that God's grace is sufficient for every aspect of your life and your victory through each trial continues to display that to the world. Your victory also displays in heaven the sufficiency of God's grace just as Job's victory did.

Another important truth to understand about trials is that in the midst of the trial, you will also be tested by your flesh and the enemy to disprove God's sufficiency. During the trial, you will be tempted to sin as a manner of escaping or delivering yourselves from the trial or in a way to deal with the emotion and struggle of it.

Some in the midst of trials have attempted to numb away the hurt, pain and fear with alcohol or drugs. Others, instead of exercising faith in God, will try to orchestrate their own deliverance. Some will just run away and attempt to avoid the problem. All of these afore mentioned are sins that resulted from them first being enticed with a solution to their problem. They were then lured away by their lust with the act of sin following quickly behind. The end result was death, which means separation. Just as those who are no longer alive are separated from us, these individuals were separated from God's presence, power and joy.

You cannot allow this loss to occur in your life nor should you display to the world that God's grace is insufficient. Although you may not feel his presence, he is present as he has promised. Call out to God for his grace, hold fast to your faith and endure.

ABOUT THE AUTHOR

Anthony Fusco has served the Lord for more than 30 years. His scope of
ministry has involved being a children's worker, teacher, Christian
school administrator, music ministry director, college dean, academic
vice-president and counselor. He believes that the Bible is a vital source
for the Christian life and from it all the answers for life's problems can
be found. His current outreach ministries are a Christian radio broadcast
entitled Lessons for the Christian Life and blog sites reaching over 30
countries.

www.ingramcontent.com/pod-product-compliance
Lightning Source LLC
Chambersburg PA
CBHW071821020426
42331CB00007B/1576